Intercepting the
Political Football

Anthony F. Loporchio, Jr.

NEWMAN SPRINGS PUBLISHING
320 Broad Street
Red Bank, NJ 07701

First originally published by Newman Springs Publishing 2020

ISBN 978-1-64801-843-5 (Paperback)
ISBN 978-1-64801-844-2 (Hardcover)
ISBN 978-1-64801-845-9 (Digital)

Printed in the United States of America

This book is dedicated to my parents, Anthony and Marie Loporchio. You endured difficult lives, losing two children and many family members to premature death. Though you both suffered agonizing deaths of your own, I can only hope you are now in a better place, looking down upon your only surviving child with smiles on your faces.

Song Lyric Credits for Chapter Title Pages

Chapter 1: Whitney Houston, "Greatest Love of All," Arista Records
 1986

Chapter 2: Jimmy Durante, "Smile," Warner Brothers Records 1965

Chapter 3: Barry Manilow, "Daybreak," Arista Records 1977

Chapter 4: Genesis, "Land of Confusion," Atlantic Records 1986

Chapter 5: Frank Sinatra, "My Way," Reprise Records 1969

Chapter 6: Mike + The Mechanics, "The Living Years," Atlantic
 Records 1988

Chapter 7: Barbra Streisand, "As If We Never Said Goodbye,"
 Columbia Records 1993

Chapter 8: Quincy Jones with James Ingram, "Just Once," A&M
 Records 1981

Chapter 9: Carly Simon, "That's the Way I've Always Heard It
 Should Be," Elektra Records 1971

Chapter 10: Lawrence Welk and His Champagne Music Makers,
 "Adios, Au Revoir, Auf Wiedersehen," Polygram
 Records 1970

Contents

Preface...9

1. Mr. Loporchio's Opus 11
2. Requiem for Abraham Maslow................................26
3. The Principals of Learning 42
4. Politics and Cream: Breakfast at the Briggs Building.................59
5. The Leadership Challenge 76
6. Parental Guidance Insisted 94
7. East Is East and West Is Definitely West...............111
8. Beware the Ides of March 126
9. Why Don't Sharks Attack Lawyers? 143
10. In There with the Kids 160

Epilogue: Moving My Cheese....................................183

Preface

TIME magazine interviewed thirteen teachers from ten different states regarding the financial challenges they faced as educators. It was fascinating to read the accounts of educators of different backgrounds, age ranges, and geographical locations. Each of the thirteen teachers interviewed had the credentials necessary to pursue other vocations, but chose to stay in education, even though they all emphasized a salary inhibition that was making it difficult for them to make a living. Employees have the right to be concerned about their compensation. I could call up my mortgage company and tell them that, although I have had great success with best practices in my classroom, I have incurred some unexpected expenses along the way. The mortgage company will still expect to be paid every month.

According to the National Center for Education Statistics, there were 3.2 million public school teachers in the United States in the fall of 2020. Seventy-seven percent of those teachers were female, and twenty-three percent were male. Ever since the birth of the public school system, the profession has always been dominated by women, but the imbalance never reached the point in which it currently stands. The first suggestion that has been brought forth regarding the perpetual exodus of males from the teaching profession is the salary consideration mentioned in the opening paragraph. There is also the sustenance of the gender stereotype labeling women as better nurturers and caretakers than men. I believe there are additional underlying causes as to why fewer men are pursuing teaching careers and more men are leaving the profession.

Another factor that is compelling educators to leave the profession is the challenges of dealing with student misbehavior and the failure of school districts to consistently hold students accountable for their actions. There was a time when the teacher had the final say in the classroom. That is no longer the case. If a teacher now takes issue with a student's behavior, more times than not, he or she either will not have support of the school administration or will face punitive action because the parents complained that the response of the teacher to the student's behavior was unwarranted and inappropriate. I feel that is especially the case when a male teacher challenges a female student's behavior. Unfortunately, there are some parents who are habitually rude, demanding, and out of line. They engage in personal attacks on teachers that demean and threaten them. Should the issue the parents are complaining about reach central administration and those parents have financial and political influence in the community, the teacher will end up in a very precarious position. The best parents are the ones who hold their own children accountable for their actions, respect the teachers' expertise, and work WITH the school to be as supportive and engaged in the child's education as possible. Unfortunately, those types of parents are now in the minority.

I had three main motivations for writing this book. One was to examine the way in which bureaucratic politics interfere with teaching and learning. In the process of dissecting the unacceptable permeation of politics into a teacher's life, I hope to provide educators with some of the warning signs to look for to hopefully avoid falling victim to a similar scenario that altered my life in 2019. Finally, for educators just beginning their careers, perhaps at a crossroad after many years of teaching, or perhaps pondering retirement, I will present the best reason for staying in the profession. We do not have capes on our backs. It is not possible to hit the bull's-eye with every student we instruct. However, there are many students who hold a sincere appreciation for the educational process. They invest in their teachers, and in addition to their own personal success, they leave an indelible impact on those who had the opportunity to be part of their lives. It will be my privilege to introduce ten such individuals.

1. Mr. Loporchio's Opus

I believe the children are our future.
Teach them well and let them lead the way.
Show them all the beauty they possess inside.
Give them a sense of pride to make it easier.
Let the children's laughter remind us how we used to be.

Before throwing me out of her office and removing me from a school I dedicated twenty-four years of my life to, my current superintendent told me that I think I'm right about everything. It was a ridiculously unfounded statement by a person I'd spent no significant time with or I'd never even had a cup of coffee with. The statement was fallacious. I've never claimed to be right about everything, and I will not make such a boast within this book text. In fact, there will be multiple instances within this book in which I will readily acknowledge mistakes I've made in my professional career. There are some things I am certain of, however. I know, for twenty-four years, I gave everything I had physically and mentally to one school and its students. I know I spent more than thirty-four thousand dollars of my own money to enhance the student experience and never once asked for any type of reimbursement. I know that, before my mother was stricken with cancer, I went twenty straight years without taking a sick day or a personal day. I know that I wrote 274 college recommendations that helped pave the way for many students to gain admission to high-profile schools. I know the difference between right and wrong. I can demarcate honesty from corruption. I understand, categorically, the distinction between purity and contamination. Most importantly of all, I am correct in my belief that just because a man had his hand bit does not diminish the man, what he did, or the reasons he did it.

I have not been able to relish in many of the peak experiences most people my age have enjoyed. My life took a different path. I have had some momentous days, however, one of which was October 3, 1989. On that day, at Mount Pleasant High School in Providence, Rhode Island, I taught my first class. It was certainly nothing for the educational archives. It was a rather prosaic lesson on Pericles and the Golden Age of Athens, delivered to a less than academically inclined audience. However, it was a decision I made earlier that morning that would remain a fervent motivation in my professional life for thirty years. I decided that in whatever program I was fortunate enough to be instructing, I was not going to be just another name on a faculty list. I was going to be impactful. I was going to be a difference maker. I was the one the boys and girls would be talking about with Mom and Dad at the dinner table.

Though I have taken my share of wrong turns, one mistake I have never made is concluding that preteens and adolescents are not astute enough to notice when teachers are not invested in what they do. When I had the opportunity to mentor young teachers or welcome a student teacher into my department, I would strongly emphasize that point in the hope that the young man or woman would seriously think about it. Quite frankly, if a teacher doesn't care about what they are doing on a daily basis, why should the students care? Often overlooked is that there are so many ways in which classroom teachers project their feelings about what they do. The concept is so much more complex than demonstrating proficiency in one's subject and being able to effectively convey information. I believe a willingness to personalize one's instruction contributes greatly to establishing the necessary connection between teacher and student. I believe teachers show how they feel about what they do by their level of articulation, the way in which they maintain their classrooms, the way they dress, and the amount of time they spend in the building before and after school in an attempt to make themselves as accessible as possible to students. If I make it clear from the first day that

I am making an investment in my students, there is a much better chance they will make an investment in me.

My first job was washing dishes for $3.45 per hour. It was hardly a prestigious position and, like most aspects of blue-collar restaurant work, quite untidy. However, I was taught at a young age that no matter what job one holds, one should put forth one's absolute best effort. I therefore aimed to be the best dishwasher the restaurant had. When I entered the education profession, I was certain I wanted to be a teacher more than I wanted to be a husband or a boyfriend. The level of dedication and commitment I put forward was never in question. I wasn't thinking about my salary. I wasn't thinking about investing in additional retirement plans. I wasn't thinking about the deals being consummated in the guidance office or principal's office. I trained myself to always be moving full speed ahead. My approach was to go as hard as I could as long as I could and hopefully produce the desired results.

Possessing admirable personal qualities is certainly a great foundation to launch a career, but an educator is also going to have to exhibit pedagogical skill to be impactful. To do that, one must understand their subject areas beyond content knowledge. My content area, social studies, is a magnificent forum, but one often looked upon as stodgy by the average student. Therefore, I immediately knew I would have to implement strategies to distinguish my instruction from what was taking place in the average classroom. I needed to make my classes exhilarating and incentive based. With extensive coursework in psychology, I was confident I could bring forth practices adolescents would find appealing. Interestingly, the first of those strategies, the one that has been the biggest staple of my teaching for my entire career, I discovered by accident.

During my first few weeks of teaching, by the time the school day was over, I would inevitably have a sore throat. When the problem did not subside, I had it examined, and I was told that the amount of speaking I was doing was far beyond what I was accustomed to and my vocal chords needed time to adjust. I was told to drink water and suck on hard candy. I got into the habit of putting a half-dozen Jolly Ranchers in my pocket to combat the discomfort. Of course, my students saw I had candy and wanted some. The fascination over receiving a Jolly Rancher was remarkable. I started packing bags of candy to take to school instead of a few stray pieces and incorporated the candy into my teaching. I started distributing candy to students who answered questions, volunteered to assist with tasks, or made any notable contribution to the class. I have maintained the practice my entire career, and it has been amazingly effective. Whether it was Jolly Ranchers, Starburst, Sunkist Fruit Slices, Airheads, Atomic Fireballs, Twizzlers, or chocolate, the psychology of the incentive for participating rose to the forefront and became a defining characteristic of a Loporchio class.

Central administrators quickly embrace trendy concepts and expect teachers to enthusiastically jump on board to show they are thinking progressively. Best practices change faster than the wind direction, and I often find myself returning to school on Monday morning waiting to hear what the initiative of the week will be. A teaching practice my district is particularly enamored with is formative assessment. Unlike summative assessment, which generates grades through quizzes, exams, portfolios, and standardized testing, formative assessment does not rely upon traditional grading to measure student growth. I often refer to it as a non-ASPEN (gradebook) way of measuring what a class has learned. Although my district latched onto the concept five to eight years ago, I have been utilizing formative assessment for almost thirty years.

When I was on the substitute list early in my career, I would either receive a call at 6:00 a.m. or the previous evening directing me where to report. The phone didn't ring every day. Sometimes it did not ring for several days. When my services were not called upon, I stayed home and became a fan of the Game Show Network. Although I was inspired by and eventually applied elements of *The New Treasure Hunt*, *Tic-Tac-Dough*, and *Sale of the Century* to my teaching, I was most intrigued by *Let's Make a Deal*. It was fascinating watching the contestants attempt to determine which door the best prizes were behind or whether or not to accept a gold watch they were offered or take "the box." Watching the show repeatedly, I discovered a way to apply its format to my teaching. I created a series of formative assessment activities that I have immensely enjoyed administering over the years. The activities have been revised and have evolved over time, but the underlying objective has remained the same. I use the activities as review assessments in preparation for a culminating text or exam. Students complete performance-based tasks, and depending on their level of proficiency, they may be invited to the front of the room to "pick a box." The boxes are of different shapes and sizes with each one containing a prize. The students know in advance that some of the boxes contain movie passes or gift cards, while the other boxes provide prizes that may not be as appealing. The fun part of the activities is watching the students decide whether or not to take the prize they have been offered, perhaps twenty points on the next quiz, or forego those points and "pick a box." I have given away many movie passes and gift cards, but also windshield washer fluid, pancake mix, a plunger, five-pound bags of rice, a soup ladle, mouse traps, a pizza dough roller, toothpaste, a cheese grater, and many other out-of-the-ordinary prizes. In addition to providing many hilarious moments, students complete the activities with a very precise knowledge of how prepared or unprepared they may be for the subsequent test.

I've been described as an ostentatious dresser. I do not possess the necessary physical attributes that often draw additional attention to an individual. However, I do like to look good. I am proud to work in a professional capacity and strive to look like a professional, not like I just finished plowing the back forty. I'm a believer in chromotherapy, the use of color to improve one's psychological disposition. I have therefore accumulated an extensive array of colored sport coats. In addition to achieving a professional appearance, wearing them is quite stimulating. The students are impressed with the variety and are intrigued by my encouragement to surround themselves with vibrant colors.

I am an emotional and sensitive man. I have never been hesitant to show emotion in front of students, nor do I regret ever doing so. I've cried at weddings. I've cried at funerals. I've cried at graduations and even when watching tear-jerking television and movie scenes. Unless I was on the phone with an administrator or parent discussing a sensitive subject, my office door was always open. Students saw that as a sign that I was an available resource to seek out if they needed support or just someone to speak to. Over the years, students did that on many occasions. Some of the things students shared with me were very intense. If they cried, I might have cried right along with them.

Many years ago, I had a female student who was unquestionably among the sweetest individuals one could meet. Always polite and friendly, she wrote out a long Christmas card thanking ME for my kindness. Unfortunately, she did not have a favorable domestic situation. She had been given up for adoption by her biological parents and had been raised by a foster family. Although her childhood and early adolescence were benevolent enough, in high school, relations reached the point in which the foster parents were only interested in the young woman to use her as a tax deduction. Having walked into my office one April afternoon and shared the story with me, she told me she wanted to leave her present household and asked me to adopt her. I was overwhelmed that she thought highly enough of me to consider me parental. I told her that, not having a wife and being out of the house for long stretches at a time, I did not feel I would be a good parent for her. Psychologically, there is a significant difference between a house and a home. A house is nothing more than a physical structure. A home is a place where family members cherish each other. They eagerly wait for each other to get home. They celebrate life together, and they support each other through the good times and the bad. I could offer the young woman a house with nine rooms, but I could not give her a "home." I also emphasized that being so close to her eighteenth birthday, she would soon reach legal adulthood and have the autonomy to pursue other options. A few weeks later, she told me she was "kind of pregnant" and wanted to get an abortion. Though I did give her my opinion, the situation was beyond my capacity as a social studies teacher. I immediately brought her to the appropriate interventionists who could provide her with the necessary guidance and consultation. She did graduate the subsequent June, and she did have an abortion. I have not had any direct contact with her since she graduated, but have taken note of the developments in her life through social media.

Another example that stood out involved a student who had a miserable experience in ninth and tenth grades and much of eleventh grade. Excessive absenteeism, disciplinary infractions, and a diagnosis of severe depression definitely placed her in the at-risk category. She decided to take my psychology class during her senior year. I had gained knowledge of this student through one of her previous teachers and information that had been provided to me by social services. I was told to expect the student to be "belligerent." From the onset of my contact with her, I did not find her to be antagonistic in any way. In fact, during the first week of school, she very politely approached me and asked for my assistance regarding having her senior portrait taken for the yearbook. At the same time, she told me she was very interested in psychology and was looking forward to taking the class. As the year progressed, her attendance was not what I preferred, but she made positive contributions to class discussions and turned in a high percentage of the work. As graduation approached, she and her classmates were required to present their digital portfolios to a panel of judges. Although there were more than thirty panels that had been created, I ended up being one of her three judges. She came in and presented a project she had completed for my class as one of her artifacts and examples of most meaningful work. She was upbeat, articulated herself wonderfully, and was exceptionally proud of what she had accomplished. It was a magnificent presentation, to the point where I was compelled to e-mail her later that afternoon to tell her what a great job she had done and how proud I was of her. She wrote a lengthy felicitation in my yearbook with the most significant words being "I learned this year that life flies by and, most of all, it is too short to be sad. I hope to come visit you five years from now finishing my master's in psychology. You inspire me!"

When school opened the following September, I received a phone call from the young woman's father. He told me that he and his wife wanted to thank me for "getting——to care about herself." He told me that, in addition to the depression, his daughter had been showing signs of being suicidal and that he and his wife had done as much as they could to improve the situation. Now, however, their daughter was taking college classes, was in a relationship, and was speaking very positively about the future. He said to me, "Mr. Loporchio, what you did was heroic." I was choked up, but did my best to get the words out and told him I'm no hero. Perhaps I was successful with his daughter because I understand survival, and at times it has been a struggle for me also. I try to be caring and smart and follow my intellect to survive. After that, I try to use my skills, training, and experience to try to make my classes as impactful as possible.

The two aforementioned stories are perfect examples of how out of touch administrators, especially central administrators, are with reality. I am specifically referring to people who bypassed the opportunity to stay in the classroom and seized the first opportunity that presented itself for a higher-paying position. They sit in their cozy offices and crave every new initiative they can promote to justify their salaries. They have become oblivious to the plight of the classroom teacher. All the anguish a student brings into the classroom, their teachers feel it also. Every pain, every anxiety, we take it home with us every night. Our ability to deal with it is among the many reasons we are so good at what we do!

I am a storyteller. I share with students things that have happened in my life, and I do so for specific reasons. There are too many students who maintain an "us against them" mentality regarding their relations with teachers. Adolescents especially don't believe that teachers can possibly understand their plight as teenagers, their trials and tribulations, and the challenges they often face to discover their identities. In many cases, teenagers think they know more than adults who have already been down the roads they are traveling. Nevertheless, I do not use the stories to consume time or come across as a comedian. I share things about my grade school experience and adult life to show my students that I do understand the weight they are carrying on their shoulders. I am a human being, not a social studies machine. If I am in the corridor and a student slashes me on the arm with a knife, I will bleed. I can be hurt too. I have been hurt on many occasions in my life. Especially in the psychology course, I feel students need more than vocabulary words on the board to understand the material. They need vivid examples to help them comprehend some very provocative and complex topics. Some of the stories I tell are quite humorous. Some are rather intense and have a serious underlying message that I am trying to convey.

When I teach abnormal psychology and analyze bullying as an abnormal behavior, I share the stories of being pushed down the stairs, almost drowning in the school swimming pool, and basically being terrorized my entire seventh grade year. In doing so, I am not hoping that someone is going to take out a violin and start playing it in sympathy. I am trying to convey that I understand the challenges of the grade school experience. I'm hoping that if I can get that message through effectively, some of the more reserved students will open up, invest in the power of psychology, and hopefully have a life-altering experience taking my class. When I taught motivation and emotion, I discussed sexual arousal and sexual behavior. They were not inappropriate topics. They were outlined very clearly in the approved Advanced Placement (AP) textbook I was using. Sexual script is defined as patterns of behavior that lead to sexual activity. I could write the definition on the board and ask students to copy it into their notebooks. Do they know what "patterns of behavior" means? To enhance their understanding, I would share a story about a man and a woman who lived next door to me. The students found the story hilarious, but it was based on actual events; and unquestionably, students understood sexual script when I was finished telling the story. I have been castigated for the storytelling. Even though everything I was discussing was specifically linked to the curriculum and I pointed out to the superintendent and her staff the exact pages in the textbook where the topics appeared, my actions were deemed "inappropriate." In addition to the formal reprimand, I was banned from teaching Advanced Placement psychology for two years. Given that I am no longer at that school, it is highly unlikely I will ever teach the course again. It was basically one student who caused the problem; but there have been countless others who have written in my yearbooks and included in personal testimonies to me how much they enjoyed the stories, benefitted from them, and developed a better understanding of what they were being taught.

The story revolving around a student who extended me effusive praise for my storytelling is an excellent example of what I am as an educator. Admittedly, I did not get off to a very positive start with this student. At the onset of my class, I did not find her behavior to my liking. To avoid the problem escalating to something more serious, I called her mother to discuss the issue. Soon later, the same parent came to school to have a staffing with all of her daughter's teachers. At that meeting, we were told that the student had a serious internal illness that might result in missing school. The mother gave a graphic description of what her daughter endured during a standard procedure. I felt terrible. I thought it was awful that a fourteen-year-old had to carry such a burden. I made the decision at that point that I was going to do everything I could to put a smile on that kid's face. With her classroom behavior having improved dramatically, she and I developed a great rapport. The academics were never in question. From the start, she was very conscientious, diligent, and ambitious. She asked many questions and was always looking to improve her academic status. As I got to know her better, I found her personality very endearing. She would regularly try to goad me into giving her class extra bonus questions on assessments. I learned that she was a big Jennifer Lopez fan. I have an autograph business on the side; and prior to graduation, I gave her an autographed picture, hoping it would put a smile on her face. I was not looking for anything in return. It was simply the way I did things at that school.

In November of 2018, I was extremely flattered to receive an invitation to spend Thanksgiving dinner with one of my students and her family. From some of the stories I shared about myself, the student learned that the vast majority of my family was deceased. After originally declining the invitation, I received an e-mail from the student's grandparents insisting that I join them for the holiday. I took some time to put that in perspective. It was a tremendous feeling to know that after only having had the student for a little more than two months, I was able to make such an impact. In the grand scheme of things, however, I did not feel it was appropriate to accept the invitation. I certainly did not want to devalue the quality of the request. I simply felt that, moving forward, it would be difficult to objectively assess the student had I accepted the invitation. In addition, given what the framework of my personal life is, I have my own personal preferences regarding how I approach the holidays. It was, however, very personally meaningful to me to be thought of in such a manner.

With another holiday in mind, it is interesting listening to people talk about the way in which they observe Lent and the steps they take to replicate the sacrifice of Jesus Christ during the forty days leading up to Easter. I know a man who makes a concerted effort to give up snacks and potato products during Lent, but eats gluttonously the rest of the year. I'm not denouncing Lent, but I don't feel one must make sacrifices to feel a sense of purpose or add meaning to one's life. I also do not believe such sacrifices should be limited to forty days. Is it not just as admirable to attempt to carry out one good deed each day throughout the 365-day calendar? The school year consists of a 180-day schedule, and I have always aimed to put a smile on someone's face at least one time each of those days. Whether it be the Jennifer Lopez autographed photo I gave to the aforementioned student, the Kim Kardashian signature I gave to another student, the countless yearbook pictures I have made available to both students and parents, lollipops, or a few simple words of praise, I do not believe kindness and self-sacrifice is strictly liturgical or reserved for a holiday season.

As will be mentioned in a subsequent chapter, I have not yet achieved the rapport with the students at my current school that I enjoyed at my previous school. However, I have not lost the ability to read people and ascertain their character. I recently had a sophomore student (Alvin) whom I am really rooting for. He's a basketball player who has already received state accolades for his talent, even though he missed a good portion of the season due to injury. In class, he definitely had a tendency to be silly; but observing him carefully, I could clearly see he had a good heart. Every time someone was in need or I called upon someone to assist, he was among the first persons to step forward. I root for someone like that. At one point in the semester, he was amazingly perceptive enough to see that I was struggling with some personal matters. He introduced me to the story of Inquoris

"Inky" Johnson, the University of Tennessee football star who now has a permanently paralyzed right arm as a result of injury. Johnson is now a motivational speaker who is known for "When God Says No," about how to deal with and sustain oneself during difficult times. Watching the video changed my perspective on many things, and I am grateful the young man referred me to it. To show my appreciation and to encourage him to strive to reach his greatest potential, I gave him an autographed photo of his favorite NBA player. He was overwhelmed by it and told me he was going to pay me back. I told him I wanted nothing in return but a promise to remain focused and to continue to try to be the best Alvin he can be.

There is a phenomenon in psychology called the self-fulfilling prophecy that I integrate into my teaching. Treat people as they are, and they will remain as they are. Treat people as if they were what they could be, and they will become what they could be and should be. I had a student who was rather lost during the first half of her high school experience. She then chose to take psychology. The power of the subject, combined with the way in which she was treated, provided her with an enlightening vision of how she wanted her life to evolve. The impact of the class was reflected in a letter she wrote to me at the end of that school year:

> Dear Mr. Loporchio:
>
> I wanted to express how thankful I am to have had a teacher like you in my high school experience. You have taught me so much that I know I'll use for the rest of my life. At the beginning of the school year, you had our class write a composition on why we wanted to take psychology. I didn't really know what psychology was for a while, but eventually I realized that it has to do with everything. At first, I took this course just to take it, and I never would have guessed how much I would take from it in the end. The class gave me something to look forward to almost every day because I knew I would learn

something new and interesting. I've never tried so hard in a class as I did in yours, so thank you for showing me what I'm capable of. I wanted to succeed very badly and from my point of view I did, all thanks to you. You do a wonderful job of keeping your students intrigued and making sure they understand every topic as much as they can. I have never seen a teacher more devoted to their job than you are, and after all the work you do you're still enthusiastic. If I could take another one of your classes I wouldn't think twice about it. I know that you're a teacher I can trust and that I can go to with anything. Thank you for being there for me. I'm extremely excited for my friends to take psychology next year so they'll understand my love for it. You helped me realize what I want to do with the duration of my life, which I was really struggling with, but now it's clear. I'll miss your stories and jokes. I don't think I'll ever be able to show you how grateful I am for everything you taught me about the world and the people in it.

By far, my favorite day on the calendar is the first day of school. I always enjoy getting my first look at class rosters. On those lists have been recognizable names, students whom I've taught in previous classes, or perhaps the siblings of students who have had me. On opening day, I eagerly await their arrival. I watch them enter the classroom, observe the expressions on their faces, and listen to initial comments they make to their classmates. It's always intriguing to look at new students and consider what avenues they will take and where they may be years later. Among our students, we hope to have some doctors, some lawyers, definitely a few teachers, but at the very least, a lot of humanitarians.

Never in my career were the aforementioned feelings stronger than in September of 2012. I had previously gained approval from the Curriculum Advisory Board to teach an upper-level psychology class. My department had not offered such a course in twenty years. We did teach college preparatory psychology, but the logistics of my department never afforded me the opportunity to teach it. After gaining approval to pursue an addition to the program of studies, I wrote an updated curriculum, promoted the course, and recruited an enrollment of fifty-six students. I took the opportunity to do something so unique very seriously. I had been certified by the College Board to teach a very high-profile course. I wanted it to be successful, to the point that the class would see a perpetually escalating enrollment. My utmost attention and concern was directed to the students I was assigned to. I will never forget that first day. After so much time preparing to implement the new curriculum, I could not wait for the opportunity to walk into the first class. In fact, doing so was so euphoric I walked out and went back in to enjoy the moment a second time. I told the students who were present that I considered the opportunity to teach the class to be among the highlights of my career. It was the first of seven consecutive years in which I taught the subject. The course eventually evolved into an Advanced Placement program, and it turned out to be among the most meaningful teaching experiences of my career. I felt I was the perfect person to teach the subject, not because of the number of credits I held in psychology, but because I had lived through and experienced many of the scenarios and case studies I would be teaching about. I felt I could introduce the students to the power of the subject through real-life experiences, and in doing so it would give them the opportunity to apply what they were being taught to their lives. Throughout the seven years, whether it was by way of class discussions or the written work students submitted, I learned a lot about my students. They learned a lot about me. I learned a lot about myself. With that teaching forum having been taken away from me, I honestly can say I miss it very much and feel a sense of great loss. I feel that course, and the way in which I taught it, helped a lot of people.

I taught psychology boldly and provocatively, but unfortunately, candles only burn for so long. We can force them to burn brighter, but that will also make them burn faster. There is an emotional price to pay for getting absorbed in what one does. Although that price may be high, I would rather pay it than be an inconspicuous candle, flickering only dimly in a corner.

2. Requiem for Abraham Maslow

Smile, though your heart is achin'.
Smile, even though it's breakin'.
When there are clouds in the sky, you'll get by.
If you smile, through your fear and sorrow,
Smile, and maybe tomorrow,
You'll see the sun come shinin' through, for you.

In Ray Bradbury's science fiction short story *A Sound of Thunder*, a man takes a trip back to the late Cretaceous Period. He is warned about the necessity of minimizing the events changed before returning to the present, since even the smallest alterations to the distant past could result in catastrophic changes in history. While there, the man accidentally kills a prehistoric butterfly. When he returns to his own time, he finds a world radically changed because of his actions. Bradbury's message is that even the smallest of actions can have serious repercussions. It has been speculated that Bradbury's premise led to the introduction of the butterfly effect theory and subsequent mathematical chaos theory. Certainly, there is a defined correlation between *A Sound of Thunder* and the behavior of high school adolescents, who succumb to compulsion, act impulsively, and fail to realize the potential ramifications of their words and actions.

Being both a student and teacher of psychology during my career has literally changed my life. It is the most powerful subject I have ever been involved with. Psychology is everywhere. Everything we do on a daily basis is connected to psychology. No other course or subject fits that description, and every high school student should complete a full year of psychology as a graduation requirement. Upon doing so, the younger generation will be primed to:

- Understand why people behave the way they do
- Improve their interpersonal relationships
- Become more productive employees in the workplace
- Develop strong parenting skills for the future
- Become more motivated to achieve their goals and objectives
- Improve their communication skills
- Improve their leadership skills
- Make better decisions
- Improve their memory
- Get better grades
- Be healthier both mentally and physically

Two questions I have often pondered while teaching at the high school level are:

- ➢ What is wrong with the teenage brain?
- ➢ Where is all the animosity coming from?

I have gained insight into those queries by studying and teaching the theories of the American humanistic psychologist Abraham Maslow. Maslow believed that every person has a strong desire to realize his or her full potential, to take responsibility for one's own life and decisions, and to develop an understanding of one's own psychological needs. Self-actualization, as Maslow referred to it, is the highest among a hierarchy of needs humans have. He felt that people are often distracted from seeking self-actualization because they too often focus on needs that are lower on the hierarchy.

Maslow believed that most people are controlled by deficiency motivation, the preoccupation with the desire for material things. Ultimately, deficiency-motivated people see life as a meaningless exercise in disappointment and boredom, and they may begin to behave in problematic ways. The deficiency may lead to a person becoming jealous and to behave in ways that aim to gain the approval of others, rather than in ways to preserve their dignity and self-respect. In contrast, people with growth motivation do not focus on what their lives are lacking, but take satisfaction from what they have, what they are, and the knowledge that they are working toward their greatest potential. Maslow proposed that a series of lower-order needs must be met before one can become self-actualized.

According to Maslow, the hierarchy begins with the basic physiological needs of food, water, and sleep—the first level. The second-level needs include physical comfort and security, shelter, and employment. The social needs are at the third level of the hierarchy and include family, lasting relationships, social acceptance, and sexual intimacy. The fourth level is the most intriguing of the hierarchy. The level includes the esteem needs of confidence and achievement, as well as the ability to respect others and gain the respect of others. It is the latter two that are often problematic for adolescents. Gaining the respect of others is the product of the ability to respect others. Gaining the respect of others is reaffirming and breeds confidence. However, if one does not treat others in a courteous and dignified manner, if one cannot bring themselves to display sensitivity for the feelings of others, one is unlikely to gain the respect of others. Moreover, if one cannot accept someone for who they are, if one desecrates diversity rather than embracing it, if one can't disagree with someone without being disagreeable, one is unlikely to gain the respect of others and, to be blunt, be worthy of the respect of others.

Self-actualization is achieved by fulfilling the prerequisite physiological, safety, social, and esteem needs. The self-actualized individual has a realistic insight into what their future holds; they do not get frustrated in the pursuit of goals; they understand that dealing with setbacks and failure, and asking for help when it is needed, is a sign of strength and not weakness; they do not allow anyone or anything to adversely affect their life; they see each new experience as an opportunity for growth, rather than a potential danger to be avoided. Why, then, are there not more self-actualized individuals? Specifically, why aren't more adolescents self-actualized? What's wrong with the teenage brain?

The frontal lobe of the cerebrum does not fully develop until one is approximately twenty-three to twenty-five years old. It is that part of the brain which is responsible for decision-making, judgment, and morality. The frontal lobe is vital for empathy, which, unfortunately, is a capacity rarely exhibited by adolescents. Without such a resource available, adolescents process information emotionally, through the amygdala. It therefore becomes necessary for parents to behave in a manner that exemplifies responsibility and an awareness of the consequences of one's actions. As will be discussed in chapter 6, parental guidance is suggested; but if it is insisted, children will be led down a path that will deprive them of the distinction between appropriate and inappropriate behavior and the knowledge of how to properly interact socially. I once had a student who frequently expressed disdain for her father within the reflective essays she submitted for my class. Privately, I asked her why she hated her father so much. Her response was "I've got no one else to hate." Where is all the animosity coming from?

Within William Golding's 1954 novel *Lord of the Flies*, there are many provocative questions that come to the forefront. Who belongs and who doesn't? Why do we exclude some people and not others? What myths and fables do we concoct to make others seem less acceptable? Why do some people believe they can gain supremacy by acting violently? In the public schools, insight into the answers to those questions can be obtained by examining a problem that occurs in almost every educational setting.

The National Centre Against Bullying defines the conduct as "an ongoing and deliberate misuse of power in relationships through repeated verbal, physical and/or social behavior that intends to cause physical, social and/or psychological harm. It can involve an individual or a group misusing their power, or perceived power, over one or more persons who feel unable to stop it from happening." The aforementioned definition clearly emphasizes the concept of "power." However, what exactly is power? Is power financial, meaning the ability to buy whatever one wants? Is power success, meaning a personal standing that allows one to choose what paths they travel? Is power authority, meaning being in a position to make administrative decisions which can drastically alter someone's life? Is it love, meaning the power to care and provide for those close to us? The fact of the matter is that every human being has power because every human being can act in ways that have a major impact on another person or group. Teachers are the perfect example. Every day we are in the classroom, what we do or don't do is going to have a deep impact on the students. What we say or don't say is likely to leave an indelible impression. That's power. In the case of bullies, however, the satisfaction they receive from physically and mentally harming others makes them feel powerful. In reality, their actions are not a sign of strength. A bully's actions are a sign of weakness. Bullies are victims of their own insecurities. To provide an example to illustrate the prevalence of bullying in the public schools, I conducted an extensive interview with a young woman whose entire twelfth grade experience was scarred by persecution and harassment. Here is her insight regarding her perception of the culture of her high school and the bullying she endured.

Part 1: The Culture of Cranston High School West

(Q) Did you generally have a good experience or a bad experience there?

(A) Overall, my experience at Cranston West fell short of the "best four years" of my life. In my time there, I went through an emotional rollercoaster. I remember my first day like it was yesterday. I walked in anxious of being judged, being liked by others, and being respected. Fortunately, for the first two years of high school I had an incredible group of friends. In eleventh grade, I had a romantic relationship with someone. I do not want to speak for him on behalf of his previous relationship, but from my perspective, the other partner was upset with the way they ended things, and took her emotions out on me. Since that day, I feared going to school with such dread. It made me resent the school itself, and it was an extremely unfit environment for me.

(Q) What is your opinion on the culture and environment of the school?

(A) In my opinion, the culture and environment of the school is not a fit, or a safe learning environment. Students cannot attend school without being judged or mocked by others. Sentences are not spoken without negativity or derogatory words. Days are not passed without fighting in the hallways or students having emotional breakdowns in the bathroom.

(Q) What did you like best about the school?

(A) When trying to answer this question, it saddens me to say all I can think about is all the bad things about the school. One specific thing that outweighed the bad was all the career opportunities and pathways students were allowed to explore. Without the Career and Technical Center, more specifically the Medical Pathways Program, I am unsure I would have ended up as a nursing major currently enrolled at the University of Rhode Island.

(Q) What did you like least about it?

(A) I am personally a positive person, but when it comes to Cranston West, I could go on forever about the things I would change. For starters, I disliked the environment and the way students treated others. If I were to be running the school myself, I would take bullying much more seriously. I would make community service a bigger part of the school. Additionally, I would try to get students more involved, have a more true spirit, and be proud to be Falcons. Finally, I would put my students' mental health above all other things.

Part 2: Bullying

(Q) You mentioned one female student was at the forefront of the bullying you experienced. In your opinion, why did she target you?

(A) In my opinion, this student targeted me out of jealousy. I had, and currently still have, a romantic relationship with her previous partner. I feel as though she had resentment towards him, and took her anger out on me. I also feel as though she did not have the proper resources, or education, to translate her emotions into something positive.

(Q) What are some of the main things she did to bully you?

(A) The bullying started off as comments attacking my persona and my appearance. She would insult me and yell at me in the hallways. The comments then escalated to the worthlessness of my being as a whole. If that was not bad enough, the student also attempted physical violence, as she attempted to run into me with her automobile. The first incident was in the parking lot of the LA Fitness Gym. My friends were telling me to move out of the way before she hit me. She was close enough to me that I felt the heat of her headlights on the back of my legs, and in the blink of an eye, she swerved away from me. A similar incident occurred in my school's parking lot. She almost hit my friend one day walking out of school, and she said to my friend, "Sorry, wrong girl," because she meant to hit me instead.

I was in gym class with her and was overwhelmed with anxiety to the point where I could not eat breakfast or sleep the night before. She would approach me in the gym locker room in a threatening manner, give me back gym stuff I let other people borrow. Bottom line, she should not have been allowed to speak to me, let alone be in a class with me. I spent most of my senior year eating lunch in the bathroom, or in my guidance counselor's office.

(Q) To whom did you first report the bullying?

(A) I first reported the bullying to Mr. Boober, who immediately sent me to Mrs. Forbes to handle the situation for him. I guess that was because the vice principals are the ones who are supposed to handle discipline.

(Q) What was the response of the following people as a result of the bullying you brought to their attention?

(A) School Resource Officer: I knew him personally because he coached my older brother's baseball team. He was not at all surprised by this occurrence. Apparently, students were bullied every day at Cranston West. He, along with the director of the Career and Technical Center, forced me to participate in a mediation session with my abuser, which sent me into a further state of heightened anxiety. The two together let my abuser yell at me during the mediation session. Neither of them being trained psychological professionals, they did not recognize the trauma it caused me, as well as letting my abuser manipulate me into thinking the whole scenario was in my head.

Assistant Principal Mrs. Forbes: She did not take care of things in the ways she promised. I was told after my first report, it would no longer be a problem, and sure enough, the bullying continued. After hearing that she and my abuser were personally acquainted, I felt as though any support she was showing for me was insincere. Additionally, she provided me with a safety pass for the hallways so that I would have to arrive to class at a different time than the rest of the students. I felt that was unfair, because I did not see why I had to change my routine, when I was the one being harassed.

Principal Boober: He acted as though he had my best interests at heart and wanted the situation settled immediately. However his actions were the exact opposite. He brushed off my issue and gave the dirty work to Mrs. Forbes. After each incident report, he never bothered to follow up, or even ask about my mental state. It pretty much showed he didn't care very much. At each school assembly he emphasized his "zero tolerance bullying policy." Anyone in that school who was a victim knows that policy doesn't exist, and is stated for the sole purpose of keeping up a good reputation.

The Superintendent: She did not meet with me personally. My mother went on my behalf with a letter I wrote to her. After that meeting, my mom said she was assured by the superintendent the bullying would stop immediately, and that I could show up to school knowing my life was not being threatened by one of my peers. My mother even stated that the superintendent was shocked at the way the school had handled the situation. Yet, for the remainder of the school year, the bullying continued.

(Q) You mentioned you were asked to participate in "mediation" to solve the bullying problem. What did they ask you to do? Were those sessions in any way useful?

(A) I was not just asked to be a participant in the mediation session, but I was told that, despite my intense anxieties, it was the only way they would take my situation seriously. As far as the actual mediation session, I was told it would only last five minutes, and that if I was at all uncomfortable, I could leave and return to class. When my abuser first walked in, she immediately asked where Mrs. Forbes was, who I had asked to be removed from the case. She sat down at a small table across from me stating that it was unfair, and accusing me of starting it over a boy. I was in such fear of her. She manipulated both me and administration into thinking I imagined the whole situation. Regardless of her manipulation, I gave both written and verbal statements reporting the abuse more than once, and the school did not even give her a single detention. The school provided me with no psychological support. A psychologist diagnosed me with PTSD. You don't typically hear of people being diagnosed with such an illness from traumas that occurred from bullying. The only PTSD I had ever heard of was from war veterans. I was astounded when I realized the seriousness of this condition. I had not previously realized how much I was affected. I knew I was not well emotionally, but I did not know that having such high anxiety for two years straight would have lifelong effects on both my physical and mental health. I should have gotten help sooner, when I was crying on my bedroom floor praying to God to make it all end. I thought long and hard about suicide. I lost more than ten pounds from not being able to eat. I resorted to pills just so I could rest my mind at night long enough for me to fall asleep. I felt weak. I felt worthless. I felt helpless. Months after graduating from high school, I still had trouble sleeping at night. I cannot have normal chemical brain levels without taking pills. I have my good days and bad days, but mostly all of them I spend questioning my worth. It has affected my relationships, friendships, and family life. The damage is done. I just hope one day someone in charge wakes up and realizes what is happening is not acceptable. Students should feel wanted and protected by their school. I cannot rewrite my story, but I will do everything in my power to possibly rewrite someone else's, and to stand up for the students failed by a broken system.

Throughout the course of my career, spanning more than three decades and multiple schools, there were certainly students in my presence I was less comfortable with than others. As educators, we realize every student we are assigned to will not be a citizenship award winner. There will always be students who pursue a different itinerary than the preferred course. However, far more times than not, students are willing to meet their teachers halfway, and we deliver them to where they need to be. One clear exception was a student I taught in an eleventh grade US history class. In all my time in public school classrooms, I cannot readily recall feeling more physically threatened than when I taught this particular individual.

Very early in the year, this male student began to demonstrate disdain for the way I conduct my class. During a discussion on the current job market, as I was expressing my belief that the average adult annual salary in the United States was scarcely enough to meet the cost of living, this student inexplicably took my comments as being a personal attack upon him. He erupted into a tirade claiming that I didn't know what I was talking about and what I was telling students was wrong and that I had no right to be giving students incorrect information. Shortly after this, on another day when he felt the need to assert himself, he said: "Don't bother challenging me because I'm a step ahead of all of you." He was referring to the staff members he felt he had the ability to outthink. The belligerent behavior continued almost on a daily basis.

While giving instructions regarding new assignments and handouts distributed to students, he told me to "calm down," rather than respectfully asking me to repeat instructions or details he did not understand. During a lunch period, he asked for a lavatory pass at the beginning of the period and was given one. Upon returning from lunch, he again asked to leave the room (to socialize with his buddies in the corridor), and I denied him the second pass. He immediately burst into another diatribe in front of the class, saying: "What's wrong with this guy? He makes no sense." He felt it was outrageous that I would not allow him to leave the room a third time after his first lavatory trip and the lunch break. On the day report cards were issued, he came charging into my classroom immediately upon dismissal. Astonished at his failing grade, he demanded an explanation as to how he could have failed the class. I was willing to calculate his grade right in front of him and did so. When he saw the numbers come up on the calculator, 58.5, he said, in a vehement, intimidating tone, "Come on. You gotta round that off to a 60." I replied that his behavior did not merit receiving that type of consideration. He stormed out of the room, cussing at me under his breath. By that point, I had documented every episode and was in communication with the guidance counselor, social worker, and administration. The bullying did not cease. In fact, it intensified for the obvious reason that every instance the student was not held accountable for his actions reaffirmed his belief that the way in which he was conducting himself was justified.

As the Christmas vacation was approaching, I gave the students an open notes test to boost their grades. Without bringing the proper materials to class, the student in question didn't have any notes to achieve what should have been an easy "100."

He started cussing. "This is BS. This is really BS."

I said to him, "Are you prepared for class? Do you have the appropriate materials with you? If not, you should not be cussing at me because the responsibility lies on your shoulders."

He then replied, "Who's cussing? BS is not cussing."

I then said to him, "I'm sorry, but I have the right to give this test."

He then yelled out, "Don't apologize!"

For the remainder of the period, he was staring me down, following me around the classroom with his eyes, obviously looking to escalate the situation further.

During the subsequent week, the final classes leading up to the holiday recess, we were watching *Schindler's List* to augment our content coverage of World War II. The first two days, he was staring at me as if he was waiting and hoping that I would confront him about not being in his assigned seat. I didn't do so because I felt it was not worth taking time away from the movie. On the third day, however, he was also encouraging other students to switch seats, again staring me down and realizing that I would most certainly respond to what he was doing. I did respond, without raising my voice and without reprimand. All I said was "Let's all sit in our correct seats today." Again, very consistent with his previous reactions to basic classroom protocol, he responded, "Okay, Mr. Loporchio, whatever you say. I just wanted to get a better look at the TV, but you obviously have a problem with it. I don't know why you have a problem with it, but you obviously do, Mr. Loporchio." At that point I directed him to report to the disciplinary referral center the school had in operation at that time. He got up and walked out, chanting, "Okay, Mr. Loporchio, whatever you say, whatever you say. Thanks a lot, Mr. Loporchio."

There was no doubt that this student fit the description outlined in the bullying policy of the district disciplinary code: "being intentionally unfriendly," "employing sarcasm," "taunting," and "threatening gestures." His behavior threatened the comfort and security of the learning environment. More important than the unnecessary grief he induced upon me, he made many responsible students in the class very uncomfortable by having to witness such consistent and ridiculous episodes. Their right to receive the enrichment the class had to offer was violated by this student. I felt he should have been removed from the class. Moreover, instead of simply transferring him to another class, I respectfully suggested he should be forced to demit the class and take the entire course over the subsequent year as a senior. Perhaps by that time he would have developed a better understanding of and respect for appropriate classroom conduct.

The student was not removed from my class. In fact, he never incurred any serious consequences for his actions. Fortunately, incidents during the second half of the year were more sporadic, and I was able to induce the student to complete enough work to assign a passing grade and bid him farewell. There was a striking commonality between the student I had difficulty with and the student who was bullying my aforementioned interviewee. In both cases, the actions of the offending student clearly fit the criteria documented in the district bullying policy. In both cases, the behavior of the victim was questioned as opposed to carrying out an appropriate adjudication against the bully. In both cases, the failure of school personnel to take appropriate action empowered the bully and led to subsequent torment for not only the victim but also the responsible students forced to bear witness to the bully's actions. I've asked some of the higher-ups why it is more likely a student will be assigned detention or suspended for being chronically late to school than incurring discipline for what amounts to, in many cases, exclusionary acts. The answer I have been consistently given is that, in this age of litigation, school districts are extremely hesitant to open themselves up to lawsuits as a result of expelling students and being sued for violating their rights and depriving them of their educational opportunities. It is inconceivable that there are an overwhelming number of people heartbroken over the rights of miscreants who disrupt a school, harass their classmates and teachers, and attempt to make a mockery of the institution of education. The district politicians are calling the shots, however. What they fail to realize is that bullying and exclusionary behavior is very much like extortion. Though there is research to support the theory that exclusionary discipline does not improve student behavior, there is also research that shows that when adolescents have proven, beyond a reasonable doubt, that they cannot or will not comply with school protocol, they are a physical and mental danger to other students and staff members and should not be matriculating at that school. The failure of British Prime Minister Neville Chamberlain and other European leaders to properly respond to the aggression of Adolf Hitler in the 1930s made World War II inevitable. When extortionists are capitulated to, they continue to forge ahead and cause further trouble.

On February 14, 2018, nineteen-year-old Nikolas Cruz killed seventeen people and injured seventeen others during a shooting spree at Marjory Stoneman Douglas High School in Parkland, Florida. Cruz had serious behavioral issues dating back to middle school. His high school classmates testified that he had anger management issues. Cruz regularly joked about guns and violence. He made threats of shooting up establishments. Cruz had accumulated a long list of disciplinary infractions including kicking doors, fighting with and threatening classmates, using profanity, insubordination, and disruptive behavior. Though he was transferred six times in three years from one school to another, legally he could not be permanently expelled. According to FAPE, enacted in 1973, "a free appropriate public education must be available to all children residing in the state between the ages of 3 and 21, inclusive, including children with disabilities who have been suspended or expelled from school." If problem students have the right to disrupt schools, without apprehension, then everyone else should have the right to an educational experience free from fear.

One of the victims of the Parkland shooting was eighteen-year-old Meadow Pollack. In a remarkably heroic display, Meadow attempted to shield a freshman female from the bullets and was shot a total of nine times. Both girls were among the seventeen fatalities. Andrew Pollack, Meadow's father, subsequently wrote *Why Meadow Died*. In powerful fashion, he illustrated how the insistence of being politically correct resulted in "the most avoidable mass murder in

American history." Meadow and sixteen others were killed by bullets, but the underlying cause of their deaths was policies, not weapons. Problem students continue to be capitulated to in order to protect the reputation of school districts. Apparently, there is too much state and federal funding available to do the right thing.

If it is not legally or politically possible to remove problem students from an educational setting, something must be done to increase the likelihood of their compliance to school protocol while simultaneously ensuring the safety of other students and staff members. Mr. Pollack and other school safety activists have proposed using metal detectors, bulletproof windows and doors, and high-profile security companies that will monitor every school and make sure kids are safe. Although those progressive measures could prove to be efficacious, they are not economically feasible. In addition, there will likely be conservative parent obstructionists who believe those measures are too radical for the public schools. Therefore, other avenues must be considered. Has anyone ever contemplated taking an academic approach to improving school safety and the overall culture of schools?

During the fifth century BC, a very wise man in Ancient Greece taught that knowledge was the most valuable thing one could possess. With knowledge, one can solve any problem. Knowledge also breeds virtue and a heightened sense of morality. If those teachings of Socrates are true, we should be able to educate our students on the challenges of adolescence. We should be able to teach students to improve their interpersonal relationships, manifest better impulse control, and lessen their reliance on the hedonistic materialism that dominates their lives. Is it reasonable to conclude that if we teach students to better understand human behavior, over time they will make better decisions? As pointed out at the onset of the chapter, a required course in psychology will foster all of those aforementioned abilities. In addition to promoting twenty-first-century skills, the drive to produce self-actualized young men and women will better prepare them to meet the challenges of an ever-changing world. A day without Maslow is no day at all. Teach him. Preach him. Then watch your kids walk tall!

3. The Principals of Learning

I'm singin' to the world. Everybody's caught in the spin.
Look at where we've been.
We've been runnin' around, year after year,
blinded with pride, blinded with fear.
I'm singin' to the world. Don't you see it all comes around?
The feeling's everywhere.
We've been closin' our eyes, day after day,
covered in clouds, losin' our way.

The best part about teaching is the privilege of being in a classroom, facilitating learning, interacting with students, and making them better persons than they were before they met us. I have never understood why a classroom teacher would dismiss those privileges in order to pursue building—or district-level administration. Perhaps they are interested in the concept of empowerment and the prestige associated with the titles conferred upon them. Are they motivated by salary increments? Do they have an innate determination and ambition to make their institutions model schools? Whatever their motivation may be, those pursuing such a path inevitably are drawn into a political forum. Since there is no place for politics in education, the tendency of administrators to be politically motivated is problematic for the faculty and staff working under them.

Current certification of a Rhode Island high school principal calls for a graduate degree and twenty-four credits of graduate coursework in school and community relations, management, curriculum development, supervision of staff and instruction, evaluation of programs, educational research, and fiscal planning. The Rhode Island

Department of Education believes such a background will allow the appointed principal to create a positive school culture and ensure the long-term success of the school and its programs. I have worked with, and under the supervision of, many individuals who attained the aforementioned credentials. Some of them were outstanding human beings and models of leadership. In some instances, I found myself questioning their priorities. Throughout my career, however, I have always tried to be respectful of the position and the title, even if I did not respect the individual person. Some principals I have worked under I did not respect as leaders, and perhaps I could not bring myself to respect them as scholars. However, I have always been cognizant of how difficult a job they have. A standard school day for all principals will most certainly include some unpleasantries, as a lot of garbage ends up on their desks.

The first principal who gained my attention I met during the course of my student teaching experience. Robert Salisbury was an interesting personality. He held a meeting with all of the student teachers on our first day. He would frequently stop in to observe lessons. He would send memos thanking us for our dedication, passion, and teaching practices he was impressed with. It was clear this man valued and emphasized the correlation between school culture and interpersonal relations. He was very concerned about new teachers on the faculty and the adverse isolation that could set in if they were not made to feel welcome and a part of the team. His approach to managing a high school was both inspiring and impressive.

In late 1991, Jerome Curzner moved from vice principal of a junior high school on one side of the city to principal of another junior high school on the opposite end of the city. He was the first principal I worked under as a contractual employee. Though Mr. Curzner advanced to the principal's chair with the reputation of being a stellar disciplinarian, his tenure as principal resulted in mixed reviews. At that time, I was a young educator with limited experience and insufficient employment references. I therefore bounced around quite a bit and invested in the department chairperson and Mr. Curzner with the hope that I might gain more meaningful employment. Going everywhere I was told and doing everything I was told,

I was a home tutor, a daily substitute, and a long-term substitute. When the long-term substitute assignment evolved into an opportunity for contractual employment, Mr. Curzner advocated for my appointment, as he then looked upon me as an energetic, diligent, and committed young educator.

The contractual employment I had attained in 1993 was advertised as temporary, and I subsequently lost the position to a veteran teacher who was much higher on the seniority list. However, when a full-time vacancy emerged in 1994, I was certain I would be appointed to the position. Having completed all of the application protocol, I interviewed for the position in the summer of 1994. It certainly was not my best interview, but I thought it was a good enough presentation of myself to gain the position. One week later, I received a call from one of the central administration secretaries informing me that I was being recommended for a .4 position. I questioned how that could be, since I interviewed for a full-time (1.0) position, and there was no .4 position even advertised. Of course, that secretary said she was "not at liberty" to discuss the matter and suggested I speak with the building principal. I went to the school to speak with Mr. Curzner that day. He said a second position, a part-time position, had subsequently been created and that was the position I was being recommended for. I certainly was interested in knowing who was being recommended for the full-time position. When told who the appointee was, I honestly had never heard of him. Upon further investigation, I was told the man had been in the system for just a few months, but played golf with Mr. Curzner. Apparently, he was also being groomed to be head football coach at one of the high schools, and it was looked upon as "advantageous" for him to simultaneously hold a teaching position within the district.

Often attributed to Aristotle, but actually the words of the American writer Elbert Hubbard, "Say nothing; do nothing; be nothing" refers to the person who intently avoids criticism because of a fear of being detracted. I am not one of those individuals. Even if the students of the full-time appointee were not reporting that their teacher could not find Mexico on a map, I still would have been quite vocal about losing out on the limited opportunity to gain full-time employment. To some, a .4 position may be considered "a foot in the door"; but to me, it was among the lowest forms of educational existence. Such a position only awarded 40 percent benefits and no eligibility to contribute to the state pension system. I did accept the position, partially motivated by the opportunity to work with some of my former teachers who were still in the building. I consulted with them often, and knowing me as they did, they were advocates of my welfare and also expressed their dissatisfaction that I did not get the full-time position. Those conversations reached the desk of Mr. Curzner. He called me in one day and told me, "It is not in your best interest to associate with those people." What principal in his right mind would discourage a young educator from calling upon his former teachers as mentors? It was indicative of the climate of favoritism and backroom wheeling and dealing that Mr. Curzner established. It did not at all surprise me when, weeks later, Mr. Curzner again called me into his office. This time he told me that he had called personnel and wanted to know why I wasn't laid off. Again, I could not figure out why a principal would say something like that to one of his teachers. I was involuntarily transferred for the next school year, and unquestionably, Mr. Curzner was influential in that decision.

On a positive note, there were instances in which Mr. Curzner's proficiency with carrying out discipline came to the forefront. I was impressed with his willingness to leave his office and tend to classroom disruptions, as opposed to simply sending the vice principal. More than once I witnessed him suspend students on the spot for infractions that merited such discipline. He was one of the few people willing to oppose a very standoffish secretary in the main office. She arrived with the school when it opened in 1954 and somewhere along the way developed an animosity toward teachers. It was the only secondary school in the district with a sole secretary working the main office. One could not pick up a stapler on the office counter without her permission. I suspected she was listening in on classroom teaching, and I successfully baited her and confirmed she was indeed doing that. Since there is to be no eavesdropping or wiretapping in the public schools, I accused her of a civil rights violation. She wrote me up to the principal, thinking he would strike the hammer down on me. To his credit, Mr. Curzner handled it quite tactfully and gave me some sound advice as to how to best deal with that secretary in the remaining time I would be working at that school. Mr. Curzner did not know it, and he will never gain the information, since he is now deceased, but his desire to remove me from his building actually propelled my career rather momentously.

When President Clinton left office in January of 2001, he had an approval rating of 66 percent. It was quite remarkable that a man who was impeached was still being endorsed by two out of every three persons who expressed an opinion. A principal whose approval rating I would estimate to be better than 95 percent was Ernest J. Logan. I was fortunate to work under him for eleven years, and although there were some challenging building issues along the way, they were enjoyable years. Although the current principal would argue other-wise, Principal Logan was the most popular principal in the school's history. The yearbook dedicated to him upon his retirement sold a school record 795 copies. Students wore T-shirts with his facial image on them at multiple events. As principal, Mr. Logan was always extremely supportive of the student body. He would frequently go into classrooms to ask students what they were working on and to take an active interest in what they were doing. The students greatly appreciated his regular attendance at athletic and social events. At the conclusion of every prom, Principal Logan would stand at the exit, wishing every couple well and imploring them to be careful on the way home. At graduation, he was known for his very emotional delivery of a poem called "The Tradition of the Rose." The door to Mr. Logan's office was always open. If a problem arose, he was always willing to communicate with his faculty in an attempt to reach an equitable solution.

Mr. Logan was a very student-centered principal. At the time, the school enrollment was consistently increasing, and the need for school management and the execution of discipline became especially important. Mr. Logan wanted the students to be happy. As much as I admire that vision for the school, there simultaneously needs to be a realization that every student will not be a citizenship award winner. Students need to be held accountable for their actions.

If not, especially within a large population, the safety of both the students and teachers becomes jeopardized. When a principal congratulates students for arriving at the auditorium in a timely manner for an assembly, it becomes clear that those students have been granted an out-of-the-ordinary leeway in the building.

One of the more memorable attempts at curbing student misbehavior during Principal Logan's administration was an initiative called "Cans for Cuts." Under this program, students who had accumulated detention hours could reduce time to serve by one hour for each canned good they donated. In other words, if Jackie Q. Student was assigned five hours of detention for throwing chocolate milk at Principal Logan (which actually happened), Jackie could have those detention hours rescinded by bringing in five canned goods. The short-lived initiative failed miserably and was generally looked upon by the faculty and staff as ludicrous. One morning in the main office, in front of a large group of people, one of the math teachers, a rather sardonic individual, said to Principal Logan, "How many cans do I have to bring in to come in late?" Though that question induced laughter from the passersby, it was also indicative of the serious deficiency the school had with carrying out discipline. By 2006, the situation became so bad that the union delegates in the building went to Principal Logan and insisted changes be made. Mr. Logan had already announced his retirement, and his successor was already making sporadic visits to the building to begin getting a feel for the school culture. That successor came into the building the subsequent September with a lengthy and rigid list of mandates. There is no doubt that those edicts coincided with observations that were made during the final stages of the Logan principalship.

Putting everything into perspective, I feel the vast majority of the teachers who were there would agree that the Logan years at Cranston High School West were good years. Although I was very taken back by a statement Mr. Logan made at a faculty meeting about parents caring more about athletics than academics, I feel there was a lot less pressure on teachers during the Logan years. Although I was confused by a notable 32 percent increase in female staff members during the Logan years, it did not affect my ability to do the things

I needed to do to carry out my responsibilities. In eleven years, I had only one intense argument with Principal Logan. When I needed his support on a personal matter that was very important to me, he provided it, without hesitation. Long after his retirement, I would frequently encounter Mr. Logan in the community or see him driving his Corvette around the city. At graduation in 2018, I had the privilege of delivering "The Tradition of the Rose" Principal Logan was known for. He had passed away the previous fall, and I was the first person to recite the poem since his death. It was a very meaningful event in my career. As I tried to emulate the emotion that was characteristic of his recitals, I was thinking about the undying passion and sentiment he held for the school. Principal Logan will never be forgotten by past graduating classes, retired teachers, or the current faculty members who were fortunate to have worked with him and known him.

The best principal I worked under in thirty-one years as an educator was Steven C. Knowlton. Granted, it was not an easy inauguration. I first encountered Mr. Knowlton at a professional retreat my school attended at the close of the 2005–2006 academic year. He made a cameo appearance at one of the daytime sessions and pretty much isolated himself from the group, with a seeming unwillingness to speak with anyone. Later that summer, I was in the building to check on some things and entered through the side door of his office to introduce myself. He did not seem particularly impressed with my initiative to meet and greet. When school started, the aforementioned edicts immediately went into effect, and admittedly I did not like the atmosphere that was being created. I felt many of the new rules were geared toward people who were unprofessional and did not do their jobs properly. Not being a derelict, I did not like being subjected to those rules. The secretarial staff thought it was wonderful that a militant style of building management was now in effect. Though I had initial doubts about this principal, I forced myself to realize that it was simply a matter of Mr. Knowlton needing time to get to know the building and the faculty. Over time, he would be able to see who the best teachers were and know who was buttering the bread so to speak. My optimistic appraisal of the new principal proved to be correct.

Mr. Knowlton was principal for six years. During that time, he observed my passion for teaching and making yearbooks. He took note of how I always put the students' needs before my own. Referring to me as "Dr.," he strongly advocated for my promotion to department chairperson in 2010. The two years I was one of his leaders were among the most enlightening of my career. Steve Knowlton was unquestionably the most intelligent principal I have ever worked under. I actually looked forward to his leadership meetings for the opportunity to gain his insight on a vast array of topics. In 2011, a supervisory curriculum position opened up outside of the building. Mr. Knowlton asked me if I was going to apply for the position. I immediately told him I wanted to stay in the building with him. The chance to work with him in a close capacity was a remarkable opportunity to add to my knowledge, and I never considered the promotional position.

When I needed to bring a matter to Mr. Knowlton's attention, I could tell he was already computing a potential solution in his head while I was outlining the issue. Unlike the other main high school in the city, Cranston West never established an archive for its yearbook materials. Not wanting to be forced to dispose of materials chronicling the history of the school because of a lack of space, I went to Mr. Knowlton to ask if there was a place in the building I could use. The very next day, he approached me with a solution. When the opportunity arose to move into a more spacious office and I needed my things moved, he left his office and walked around the campus in the summer heat and humidity in order to find custodians to help me relocate. Mr. Knowlton greatly valued his department chairpersons. He listened to our appraisal of building issues and welcomed our input. Although we had a strong relationship with this principal, that did not mean he was easily satisfied. He was the toughest evaluator I ever had. He was not easily impressed when observing a lesson. He was never hesitant to pull one of us aside and tell us that he did not agree with the way in which we handled a situation. I never minded any of that, as I always knew where I stood with him.

When we needed his support, however, we always had it. I recall an instance when I had a personal matter I was struggling with. Mr. Knowlton sat in my office for an hour, listened, and sincerely attempted to assist me during a time of need. His support was also evident during an absurd episode that occurred during the final year of his principalship.

In 2011, the district adopted a new teacher evaluation model. The model was complex to the point where all curriculum leaders had to complete five days of training to prepare for the implementation. The training was to take place outside of the school. Neither I nor the other four department chairpersons were opposed to the model or the training. However, we were collectively concerned about being out of the building for a full week. We felt it would be especially inhibiting to lose so much teaching time in the upper-level classes we instructed. We inquired through our main union delegate if there was a way we could complete the training without losing so much instructional time. For some reason, what was meant as a polite inquiry was looked upon as a mutiny by central administration.

Monday morning, September 12, 2011, was bright and sunny outside of the school; but it quickly became dark and gloomy inside the building. While we were teaching our period 1 classes, all of the department chairpersons were called to the main office. We were then brought to the guidance conference room where the then superintendent, the curriculum director (the current superintendent), and Mr. Knowlton were already seated. As she has a tendency to do, the curriculum director immediately took over the meeting and excoriated us for questioning the district initiative of completing training for the implementation of the new teacher evaluation model. In an elevated voice, she made it clear that it was not our place to question anything from central administration. We would do as we were told, and that's all there was to it. The other department chairpersons and I were rather astounded that a minor inquiry could result in being pulled from our classes to be verbally reprimanded. Principal Knowlton sat silently through the indictments and was clearly uncomfortable with what was transpiring. He would later go on record as saying, in reference to his five department chairpersons, "This is the best group I've ever worked with."

I honestly believe that what happened on September 12, 2011, influenced Mr. Knowlton's decision to leave the district. To be forced to sit and watch his five curriculum leaders be spoken to like children over something so petty was indicative of the way in which central administration was being run and the direction the school department was moving in. As a veteran educator of more than thirty years, he did not have to accept the platforms of those central administrators. He announced his departure the subsequent spring, and I was perhaps the one hurt most by his retirement. I felt a sense of great loss. It was a privilege to work for Steven C. Knowlton and be a beneficiary of his knowledge. If he had asked me to sell popcorn at the Friday night football games, I would have done so. That is the level of respect I held for that man. I will always be grateful to him for the role he played in the advancement of my career and will remember him through the final written words he sent me:

> I enjoyed working with you in all capacities. I always knew that whatever you were involved in would be done in a timely manner and always done thoroughly and professionally. I was very fortunate and blessed to work with such a great leadership team that was so invested, committed, and professional. You and the others at CHSW made me look good. Thank you for everything. STEVE

While I was directing the project that produced the fiftieth anniversary yearbook for Cranston High School West, I had the privilege of gaining the insight of Mr. Joseph Coccia. I had never previously met the man who was principal of the school from 1962 until 1982. "Joe Rock" as he was called, he once reprimanded a teacher for moving a typewriter without written authorization. With such a reputation preceding him, I was afraid to even call him. However, I was certain his knowledge of the early history of the school would prove to be invaluable. I decided not to risk a stern response to a phone call and opted for e-mail communication. Mr. Coccia responded to my e-mail in less than an hour. Not only was he interested in the project; he insisted we meet to discuss the particulars. After a first meeting of four hours, he invited me to his house for a follow-up session. Although this eighty-seven-year-old man had failing hearing and failing eyesight, he also had a memory as sharp as a tack. He exhibited a passion for education and much fervor for promoting and preserving the culture of a school, and its history, far beyond anything I had ever witnessed from an administrator. The knowledge gained over the course of six hours was fascinating. From why the school was built to the choice of school colors and a mascot to the story behind a controversial prayer banner a student would litigate against years later, Mr. Coccia was a wealth of information who was proud of the role he played in the early evolution of the school. It was also clear that he was very much elated that he was not only remembered but also being asked to contribute to a project he so personally valued. There is something to be said for letting impactful people know they have not been forgotten after they have left a program and are traveling down different roads.

On Thanksgiving Day of 2019, I received a call from a friend who has a child at Cranston High School West. He was in attendance at the holiday football game and called to tell me that the principal was walking up and down the sidelines of the stadium attempting to gain recognition and approval from the crowd. Within the upcoming text, it will become clear why I no longer have ties to that principal; but, at this point, I can honestly say that what was witnessed on that Thanksgiving morning sums up the persona of Theodore Boober perfectly.

Although it would be many years before I got to know him well, I first met Theodore Boober in 1991. We were both substituting at one of the junior high schools, and like myself, he was a social studies teacher. Always being a street-smart individual, he took note of the poor job prospects and moved into special education, where there has never been a shortage of employment opportunities. He subsequently pursued a career in administration, and I saw very little of him until he did a one-year stint at Cranston West as vice principal. He became a middle school principal immediately thereafter and remained in that capacity before succeeding Mr. Knowlton in the summer of 2012. A colleague of mine worked with him for several years at the middle school and correctly predicted that he and I "would not hit it off."

Regardless of what I've heard about staff members and students before I work with them directly, I believe in beginning working relationships with a clean slate. I pass judgement on no one until I have enough firsthand experience with them to properly assess their character. On July 26, 2012, I went into the school to have an initial conversation with Principal Boober. My goal was to establish a foundation for positive communication moving forward. To break the ice, I brought in a fifteen-inch zucchini I had harvested in my backyard and presented it to him. After a rather prosaic opening to the conversation, he told me there was something he needed to speak to me about. He closed the door and proceeded to tell me that during his final conversation with the outgoing principal, Mr. Knowlton expressed serious concerns about my behavior and suggested to Principal Boober that it was in the school's best interests that he be mindful of it. As previously mentioned, Steve Knowlton did not work that way. If he had been concerned about the way I conducted myself on his staff, he would have addressed the issue with ME, not Theodore Boober. Principal Boober must have known I would easily be able to expose him as a liar. Nevertheless, he decided to take a classless approach to an initial conversation with one of his department chairpersons, one with seventeen years of pristine service to the building. When I contacted Steve Knowlton about the allegation, he told me he never had such a conversation with Principal Boober.

When school opened in September, Principal Boober's anxiety about managing a building five times the size of his previous school immediately came to the forefront. It took him until December to realize that he should regularly meet with the department chairpersons to discuss not only curriculum matters but also all aspects of the building's management. When those meetings commenced, he would regularly take jabs at the previous principal about all of the problems he thought he inherited. He seemed to resent the fact that the five department chairpersons had a very positive relationship with the previous principal. I particularly detested a commitment he made to the parents to become their personal hero. Every concern a parent brought forward was granted the utmost credence. Moreover, Principal Boober established informants on the faculty, most notably a guidance counselor, who would tell him about things other teachers were saying and doing. He would then approach those teachers and challenge them with the allegations. The school climate for the 2012–2013 year was very noxious. It was the result of a principal who was very frantic and very unsure of his ability to manage the building. During that time, I did not gain Principal Boober's esteem. At the end of that school year, he saw an opportunity to strike the hammer down upon me.

For the 2012–2013 academic year, I piloted three sections of honors psychology. I had a student who missed fifty-five classes due to illness. Though I was able to get her through with a "B+," she and her parents felt the grade should have been an "A." When I did not submit an "A," the family accused me of a 504 violation. Such an allegation is a building issue. The parents came into school for a meeting with Principal Boober and a subordinate administrator. If I had been invited to that meeting, I gladly would have outlined the steps I had taken to meet the mandated accommodations of the 504 plan. Instead, Principal Boober and his subordinate encouraged the parents to file a formal complaint at the superintendent's office. I know that to be true. I was summoned to the infamous Briggs Building, which will be thoroughly described in the next chapter. While I should have been attending a meet and greet at the incoming freshman hot dog roast, instead I was giving a deposition in the superintendent's office. In order to do so, I was entitled to a copy of the formal complaint. The parents put in writing that they had filed the complaint as a result of a meeting they had with Principal Boober and Mrs. Mangione. Though I was easily able to fend off the allegations and show that I had not violated the 504 plan, I should not have been subjected to such a meeting, nor should I have been subjected to the one-year probation I was placed on.

Theodore Boober is indeed an intriguing personality. Called "The Fudd" by those who worked with him at his middle school, he is by no means a scholar. He is more likely to be seen on *The Gong Show* than *Jeopardy!* He mispronounces terminology and uses other terms out of context. He surrounds himself with people who will work hard, be company men and women, and make him look good in the process. Nevertheless, after two turbulent years, I found myself really wanting to have a quality relationship with him. I found myself daring to believe in his platform of bravado and pomp and circumstance. He is definitely the biggest cheerleader for a school I have ever seen. He always has the current yearbook conspicuously displayed on his desk. There are not likely too many schools that have the marching band, precision dance team, and flag corps meeting the parents at the front entrance at open house. Seeing those things is exciting and compels one to want to contribute to them. I honestly tried to do so and, in the process, foster a relationship of mutual respect. As a senior teacher and a member of the leadership team, it was my responsibility to support the principal's platform. I therefore always made myself available when he needed me. I was giving him Christmas gifts and regularly bringing him the Greek spinach pies (spanakopita) he had an appetite for. Unfortunately, there were always things that got in the way of the good tidings, usually things connected with his fear of the superintendent and, to a much greater extent, his incessant need to be a hero to the parents of the community and his need to be at the center of attention.

Principal Boober likes publicity, and he relishes the opportunity to gain media coverage for the school and its events. In January of 2016, the city initiated a program connecting high school students with senior citizens who needed help shoveling snow during the winter. A press conference was held at the city senior center to recognize the students involved. The director of the city's senior services had a man dress up as an elderly woman and attend the press conference. The man was wearing a gray-haired wig, lipstick, glasses, earrings, and a tag on his lapel saying senior home resident. The motivation for that action was later revealed to be the desire to achieve a better presentation for the local media. The image of the disguised individual went viral on social media. Right behind the man was Principal Boober, totally oblivious to the fiasco that had been made from what should have been a very heartwarming story. Why was Principal Boober in the picture in the first place? The press conference was meant to recognize senior citizens and high school students performing community service. There were no senior citizens or students in the photo that got the most publicity. Instead, Theodore Boober's vanity and need for attention resulted in him looking quite foolish.

In September of 2016, a high-profile student athlete arrived at Cranston High School West. His father is an icon in the Rhode Island Interscholastic League. That parent, though not a school faculty member, was very interested in an expeditious acceleration of his son's athletic resume. The parent was looking to be a "consultant" to the varsity team his son would be playing on. The coach of that team, although not opposed to gaining input from a coaching icon, had a full assistant staff in place and did not see the need for an additional person. Principal Boober was well acquainted with the iconic parent, to the point in which they took vacations together. Principal Boober used his influence to attempt to increase the role of the iconic parent on and off the practice field. Not able to succeed, the decision was made to remove the varsity head coach from a position he had held for more than twenty years. Granted, that particular team had not won a championship since 2004, but there were far better ways to enact a coaching change than what was done. The head coach could have been asked to consider a successor and perhaps slowly integrate that person onto the coaching staff. To call someone into an office on a Friday afternoon and fire them is just another example of how the principal's municipal relationships, and need to be exalted by parents, interfered with a staff member's career. It was not the first time it had happened, and it would not be the last.

The career, and life, that was the most disrupted during the principalship of Theodore Boober was unquestionably mine. As it will be fully documented in chapter 8, my decision to take issue with a student's behavior resulted in losing a leadership position, four supporting roles, and almost seven thousand dollars of annual gross salary. When I was removed from the building after what should have been a very black-and-white disciplinary adjudication, Principal Boober thought there was no chance I would be returning. The day I did return, he came running up to my office, threw his hands into the air, and pleaded the Fifth Amendment regarding the role he might have played in my removal from the school. At that point he pledged to be my personal Lancelot should I have a need. As it will be documented in chapter 8, there were a lot of very bad things taking place, especially in regard to central administration's capitulation to two country club parents who had threatened to file a lawsuit and report their concerns to the local news media. I was informed that the student involved was not going to attend my Advanced Placement psychology course. She was not going to turn in assignments. She was however going to be assigned a grade of "A" for the course.

As much as I respected Principal Boober's cheerleading for the school and emphasis on the promotion of school culture, I felt academic integrity still must come to the forefront. If an institution of learning, especially one that has been designated an accredited four-star school, does not have academic integrity, it has nothing. I did not feel it was in any way equitable, or ethical, for a student to be granted a waiver when there were 114 other students in the class who were attending, were submitting assignments, and were not being granted that consideration. I therefore refused to comply with the "directive." Immediately thereafter, Jim Torres, the curriculum supervisor for my content area and a personal friend of Principal Boober, was given access to my grading portal. Since I was not willing to provide the offending student with what was demanded, Mr. Torres would do so on the school's behalf.

On Friday afternoon, May 17, 2019, I was passing through the main office and noticed Theodore Boober and Jim Torres having a conversation in the principal's office. When in closer proximity, I overheard my name and went into the office to take issue with the obvious wheeling and dealing that was occurring. I made it clear to Principal Boober that if he had a directive from central administration regarding me, he was to come up to my office and discuss it professionally or invite me down to his office for that purpose. I told him to knock off the backroom wheeling and dealing and, to quote my specific words, "Cut out the clandestine crap!" Before exiting, I told Mr. Boober and Mr. Torres that a lot of people really need to clean the deluge of soot off their knees from being down on all fours trying to accommodate a student and two parents who were totally out of line. Two school days later, I was permanently removed from the building. Following my removal, I received two communications from Principal Boober. He did not contact me to express concern or regret over what transpired. He did not thank me for twenty-four years of service to the building and the indelible imprint I left behind. He did not wish me well. He e-mailed me asking where the yearbooks were and to ask me to return a chromebook he believed I walked off with. He subsequently suggested to another staff member that I embezzled funds from the yearbook activity in order to fund other programs in my department. Shame on Theodore Boober.

More than one person has asked me, "Why didn't you just give the kid an 'A'?" I didn't just give the kid an "A" because it would have been wrong to do so. More than one hundred students had put their faith in me to teach them Advanced Placement psychology, a school record for an AP course. In addition to sacrificing my own personal integrity, I was not going to disrespect many hard-working and righteous students who signed up for my class, in lieu of another course they might have taken, because they were confident I would enhance their junior or senior year. Though it is true that I failed to shield myself from much aggravation and I failed to intercept the political football, I certainly was able to maintain and, in all honesty, enhance my understanding of the principals of learning.

4. Politics and Cream: Breakfast at the Briggs Building

There's too many men, too many people,
making too many problems,
and there's not much love to go around.
Can't you see this is the Land of Confusion?

I n *Star Wars: Episode IV*, Luke Skywalker and Obi-Wan Kenobi make their way from Skywalker's home planet of Tatooine to Alderaan by way of Mos Eisley Spaceport. Kenobi warns of the need to be cautious by telling Skywalker, "You will never find a more wretched hive of scum and villainy." I will hesitate to apply such an abhorrent description to the central administration of my current employer; however, if these people express an interest in doing you any favors, give yourself an adequate opportunity to get out of town.

The campus of the city's oldest high school dates back to the late nineteenth century. With only modest and sporadic updates and renovations since, the physical plant cannot comfortably accommodate a present enrollment surpassing 1600 students. The second and third floors of the administration building house additional classrooms, while the first floor is reserved for the superintendent and her support staff. In most municipalities, key officeholders include the mayor or town administrator, police chief, fire chief, city engineer, and city solicitor. In the city of Cranston, Rhode Island, the collective salaries of those positions are not commensurate with those of the ones currently residing the first floor of the school administration building. As this chapter evolves, the recklessness and futility of allowing individuals to have and maintain positions for self-empowerment will become clear. When a person is granted a majestic title with an inflated salary, he or she will inevitably conclude they have the autonomy and impunity to play God. Magnanimity, however, is a virtue, not an entitlement.

In thirty-eight years, I have had three positive experiences in the Briggs Building. During the 1982–1983 school year, I had a Spanish class on the third floor which provided me with both academic enrichment and personal growth by way of an out-of-the-box and somewhat frivolous, but nevertheless very effective, teacher.

In July of 2010, I was invited to the superintendent's office for a second interview, as I was hoping to become social studies department chairperson within the school I was teaching at that time. The first round of interviews had been conducted internally at the high school by the principal and an additional committee of five. The top three scorers advanced to a follow-up interview with the superintendent and his support staff, one of those dignitaries being the current superintendent. I had never met her personally, but it is quite amazingly ironic that a woman who once fervently recommended me for the position would spitefully remove me from that same position years later.

After exchanging pleasantries with the interview committee, the superintendent quickly pointed out that, although I was the top scorer coming over from the first round of interviews, it meant absolutely nothing on this day. There was no constructive purpose for that comment. If I were to speculate what the objective might have been, I would say it was a psychological ploy to unnerve me in favor of one of the other finalists, a personal friend of the superintendent and a man who was then, and still is today, firmly union entrenched and politically active. The superintendent was not aware that I had prepared for both rounds of interviews in a way that no candidate for a teaching and leadership position had ever done. The result was two flawless performances, the two best professional interviews of my career. The current superintendent, then curriculum director, remarked, "Do you think we can find someone more passionate?" Of course, few candidates leave an interview with a decision. The interview committee "gets back to you." I remember exiting the Briggs Building and walking through the parking lot quite satisfied with myself. I was not assured of obtaining the position; but I was certain that, had I failed, it was not going to be because I flubbed the interview. Less than thirty minutes later, while at my parents' house for lunch, I received a call from the superintendent telling me I had a "terrific interview" and that he would be recommending to the school committee that I be appointed to the position. It was a great moment for me and my family and definitely an occasion in which I intercepted the political football.

While overseeing the curriculum during my first year as social studies department chairperson, I took note that, although students were being offered a wide array of courses, one opportunity conspicuously absent was an upper-level psychology course. We were teaching college preparatory psychology, but we did not offer a course that would specifically appeal to our Advanced Placement and honors students. Many of those students were pursuing college and university programs, and eventual careers, in fields directly connected to the central question in psychology, WHY DO PEOPLE BEHAVE AS THEY DO? I communicated my proposal to Dr. Nancy Sullivan, an adjunct curriculum and digital portfolio advisor and a former professor at Rhode Island College with whom I had completed ten graduate credits. In addition to being called upon for her valuable knowledge of curriculum and its implementation, Dr. Sullivan communicated to me that it was an especially good feeling to be collaborating on a curriculum endeavor with "one of her own." With Dr. Sullivan's guidance, I completed all of the required protocol for an addition to the program of studies and prepared to present the completed curriculum to the Curriculum Advisory Board, which held its meetings at the Briggs Building. The board unanimously voted in favor of the proposal; and, for the first time in twenty years, an upper-level psychology course was taught during the 2012–2013 academic year. The only brief hesitation to approval came from the then curriculum director, now superintendent, who had doubts that a sufficient number of students would enroll to allow the course to run. She cryptically predicted no more than ten or fifteen students would enroll. The first year saw fifty-six students enroll, with annual increases as the course evolved into an Advanced Placement forum in 2016. The enrollment for Advanced Placement psychology for the 2018–2019 academic year was 115 students.

Having previously had only those three positive experiences in the building, I was not feeling particularly euphoric when unexpected and grotesque circumstances assigned me there for the 2019–2020 academic year. Having taught there for just a brief period, it is premature to pass judgement on the quality of the experience. I do find myself having difficulty dismissing indignation. Having been ejected from a school in which I was a department chairperson, an Advanced Placement instructor, a curriculum leader, a NEASC chairperson, and a yearbook advisor, the only capacity I currently serve in is that of remedial social studies teacher. In the course of carrying out my responsibilities, I am forced to walk by the vehicles and first floor offices of the people responsible for my demotion. Mos Eisley Spaceport that first floor is not. One's experience there will quite likely equate to a combination of the Department of Motor Vehicles, the dentist's chair, and one's personal Gethsemane.

Timing is everything. In July of 1990, the General Assembly made early-retirement incentives available to eligible employees in the Rhode Island Employees' Retirement System. It was a very appetizing invitation that many teachers accepted. With twenty-eight years of service, an educator as young as fifty could retire with a 60 percent benefits package. While collecting those dividends, the retiree could get a job in the private sector to augment his or her income. It is easy to understand why there was a mass exodus of public school teachers in the summer of 1990. As a result, there were many vacancies to fill. Unfortunately, having completed my undergraduate work earlier that year, I did not have the exposure or necessary references to be seriously considered for a position.

When a teacher is unable to obtain contractual employment, he or she may opt to substitute on a daily, short-term, or long-term basis until something more tangible arises. I did that between 1990 and 1994, for almost six hundred school days, in three different communities. Although my background was in history, geography, and psychology, I found myself often teaching mathematics, English, physical education, and, on one occasion, microwave safety. I was part of a sizeable group of social studies teachers who entered the job market simultaneous to the 1990 retirement incentive. It would take a considerable amount of time for full-time job opportunities to present themselves. A colleague and I would attend the annual job fair to monitor the movement of the veteran educators. We often would speak to the assistant superintendent at that time to gain her insight on the direction she felt the job market was taking in the city. Very consistently, she would tell us, "You gentlemen are both in line for a position, but don't forget Steve Maxwell. When considering the people in social studies who are gaining exposure, you both are on the list, but don't forget Steve Maxwell. You and Peter will definitely be considered, but don't forget to put Steve Maxwell on the list." My colleague and I could never figure out who Steve Maxwell was. We had been substituting in all of the secondary schools, but neither one of us had come into contact with Steve Maxwell. Steve Maxwell did not attend the job fairs. Whoever Steve Maxwell was, he had already gained the undying affection of the assistant superintendent. As it turned out, either the assistant superintendent was an extremely prescient visionary or Steve Maxwell was a relative of an iconic member of the central administration with the same surname. Steve Maxwell enjoyed an expedited acceleration through the ranks and currently holds a prestigious leadership position.

After completing a long-term assignment in the spring of 1993, my name inexplicably disappeared from the personnel records the subsequent September. As a young teacher, one hopes to get not only the proverbial foot in the door but also hopefully a wrist and elbow. Such an opportunity came my way during the winter of 1993. A social studies teacher at a junior high school in my district decided to leave the profession. He abruptly resigned and moved to Florida to pursue an alternative lifestyle. I was asked to immediately step in and teach the five classes he left behind. At the onset, my status was "long-term substitute," and I worked per diem.

Being that it was obvious the original teacher was not coming back, the job was eventually posted, and I was contractually appointed after an admittedly perfunctory interview process. I finished out the remainder of the school year with full knowledge that the position would have to be "posted" at the June job fair. At the event, the position was taken by a veteran high school teacher, and I was reverted back to the substitute list. Although I had made it clear I was ready, willing, and able to serve in that capacity, I was not called upon during the subsequent September. I was not overly concerned at first, since good teacher attendance at the beginning of the year would usually limit opportunities anyway. As the calendar moved into October and I was still not getting called, I decided to pay a visit to the personnel office. Upon doing so, I was told I was not on the substitute list. In fact, they did not know who I was and had no recollection that I recently finished the year at one of the junior high schools. To me, it was inconceivable that I could so quickly become a nonentity after serving in various capacities for three years. I was vocal enough about my displeasure that the personnel director came out of his office to intervene. It was at that point I realized that there was something very disquieting about the Briggs Building and its officeholders. My intuition told me that I was not destined to have many pleasant experiences there. I did consider requesting to speak at the October school committee meeting, but being in graduate school at the time, I decided to dedicate my full attention to my coursework.

I was eventually "reactivated" on the substitute list and accumulated a total of 511 service days before being appointed to a two-fifths position and subsequently a permanent full-time position. Other than some minor housekeeping details, I did not have cause to be in the Briggs Building for several years. Its personnel came to the forefront in an event which was referred to by many veteran teachers as "The St. Valentine's Day Massacre." The entire union membership was called to an assembly hall for an unexpected contract extension ratification vote. We were aware that the current agreement would be expiring on August 31 of that year and negotiations were taking place, but we hardly expected to be voting on anything in February. People were immediately asking, "Why today, Valentine's Day? We can't do this next week or the week after?" A large percentage of the membership did attend the meeting. We were provided with literature that summarized some of the main features of the proposal. After brief remarks from the union president and officers, the vote was called! The audience was astonished, as standard protocol called for anyone to be able to approach the podium, ask a specific question, and get a specific answer. Questions were not being entertained. The union president kept reiterating, "This is absolutely the best deal you are going to get." The vote was again called, and the other union officers seconded the motion. Though there were people who voted NO and others who abstained, the proposal was ratified.

There were two factors that contributed to such a rapid ratification. First, there is always a large contingent of people who do not particularly care about the specifics of contract language. Their employment, salaries, and benefits are their primary concerns. The opportunity to extend those securities for three additional years often induces an expeditious approval. Second, on Valentine's Day, most people are not thrilled about sitting in a long drawn-out meeting when they have afternoon and evening plans with their spouses and children. There was no viable reason why the meeting could not have been held a week or even a month later. It was widely believed that an observance day was chosen as a psychological ploy to accelerate approval of the proposal. What none of us new at the time, however, was that the union president was planning to leave the union, and his teaching position, in order to become personnel director. It was the general consensus that, in the process of switching to "the other side," especially in such a clandestine manner, the union president betrayed the membership and compromised the integrity of the process and the positions of his fellow educators he was leaving behind. It was a typical Briggs Building transaction.

Perhaps one of the motivations for our union president switching teams and going to work at the Briggs Building was financial. The numbers were lower at that time; but presently, the building certainly does pay well, as illustrated by statistics from the school department's budget report for 2019–2020.

SCHOOL DEPARTMENT POSITION	ANNUAL SALARY
Superintendent	$175,100
Assistant Superintendent	$135,000
Chief Financial Officer	$118,965
Executive Director of Human Resources	$116,905
Executive Director of Educational Programs and Services	$116,905
Executive Director of Special Education Programs	$116,905
Executive Director of Student Information	$116,905
Management Information Systems Director	$94,300
Technology Services Director	$94,300
Evaluation Coordinator	$91,121
Athletic Director	$90,000
Data Manager Help Desk Specialist	$70,000
Payroll Supervisor (two persons)	$65,188 each
Benefits Supervisor	$64,063
Grant Fiscal Agent	$60,002

In addition to the fifteen premium positions, there is a group of administrative assistants (secretaries) allotted into the budget at $661,572 and a long list of other positions bringing the overall annual Briggs Building payroll, conservatively, to $3,480,770. Hypothetically, if an efficiency expert was to spend a week at the Briggs Building dissecting each and every one of the positions and correlating the salary the officeholder carries with the job description, would he or she reach the conclusion that some, perhaps many, of the positions are unneeded and not economically feasible? Might the taxpayers of the city of Cranston, especially those living on the western side of the city where the property taxes can easily range from $7,000 to $9,000 a year, feel it is in their best interest to have such an audit performed? Might the taxpayers ask some additional questions if they had the opportunity to compare the aforementioned salaries with the following municipal positions? According to a 2019 report prepared for the governor by the Rhode Island Department of Revenue—Division of Municipal Finance, additional principal positions in Cranston, Rhode Island, carried the following base salaries for the fiscal year ending 2018:

MUNICIPAL POSITION	ANNUAL SALARY
Police Chief	$121,092
Fire Chief	$112,799
City Engineer	$97,869
City Solicitor	$95,000
Mayor	$80,765
City Clerk	$77,180
Chief of Staff	$72,873
Tax Assessor	$67,665

In any school department administrative, the person most at the forefront and in the limelight is the superintendent, who oversees the daily operations and the long-range planning of a school district. I received my entire grade school education in Cranston, Rhode Island; and during that time, we only had one superintendent. In fact, the man was appointed five years before I started first grade and was still in the position three years after I graduated high school. During his tenure, he established committees at his schools in which he would sit down with teachers to address issues brought forth and LISTEN to their concerns. I remember being in sixth grade and being part of a group that sat down with the superintendent as he LISTENED to us describe our experience in the school. How many superintendents do that today? Since that time, we have not had the same person in the superintendent's chair for more than nine years. In one instance, the school committee brought in a candidate from Waterloo, Iowa. She was interviewed twice, once publicly and once privately, and eventually was appointed to the position. Sixteen months later, the woman resigned and would subsequently file a lawsuit against the city for breach of contract. From 2006 to 2015, we had three consecutive superintendents who served three years each. The current superintendent was appointed in April of 2015, and her ascension to the position was quite remarkable. She was a high school administrator from 2001 to 2008. She then left the district for two years to become principal of one of the top high schools in the state. In the summer of 2010, she returned to Cranston and was appointed executive director of educational programs and services. Less than five years after that, she became superintendent and the city's highest-paid municipal employee.

What is especially disquieting about the superintendent's appointment is not necessarily the employment record or credentials of the candidate, but the way in which the process was carried out. At the time, the school committee made the decision to forego a candidate search and to not post the position. A long-time member of the school committee was quoted as declaring their choice candidate a "loyal scout," and therefore a candidate search was unnecessary. The woman may or may not be a "loyal scout," though personally, I don't consider someone who leaves an employer after seven years to pursue a higher-paying position elsewhere loyal. Furthermore, I feel it is very reasonable to expect not just an interview process but also an intensive and thorough candidate screening for a position that now pays $175,100. In order to become social studies department chairperson, I had to complete two rounds of interviews. I worked with a physical education teacher who interviewed to become assistant football coach. When the head coach was fired, he was required to reinterview in order to keep his position. He had to interview twice for a position that carried a $4,000 stipend. With those types of rules in place, the school committee should certainly not be settling on one candidate while simultaneously depriving the tax-paying community the opportunity to play a role in the process. Transcripts from the social media outlet BASICS (Benefiting All Students in Cranston

Schools) clearly indicate there was much consternation regarding the appointment of that superintendent and the way in which any formal process was being disregarded:

DM: That is very disappointing. No search committee? No public input?

PM: Wow, UNREAL.

JR: Another fast one? At least post, search and interview. Even it turns out that's the best option they need to follow the process right.

JA: ALL POLITICAL BS NOTHING CHANGES

DM: Politics as usual in Cranston. Does anyone know if we have any recourse? If not, time to clean house come next election.

MWT: When my mother was head of the school committee it was a huge process to hire a superintendent. It took months of interviews and even traveling to other states to interview if necessary. There was always more than one candidate. I've never heard of someone just being appointed.

KTB: I would assume this is meant to be an interim position.

KK: If it is supposed to say "interim" someone better correct this agenda ASAP. I get emails from the Secretary of State, so if the agenda is changed I will post on this feed ASAP. If it isn't an irresponsible oversite, I hope your all join me at this meeting to voice your anger and displeasure.

DM: We DO have recourse. We all go to this meeting and demand a search.

MF: This is so VERY disappointing! Do we the tax payers have zero input?? It's an outrage!!

KK: For anyone wondering, it was NOT supposed to say interim…she is going to be made the Superintendent with no search, no posting.

BFK: Unbelievable. Truly disappointing.

MG: Quick, everyone act surprised!

KK: Really, I think we sit and talk on Facebook, but this is the time to get out there and get to a meeting… Tuesday night. Parents need to show up. At the least, email the school committee and tell them this is not ok.

JR: Can you post the emails for everyone to write the school committee?

JR: I would really like to think it's an interim position.

KK: Jim, it is NOT an interim. I have confirmed this. 100 percent not interim.

DM: I did just send a very strongly worded email to my Ward 6 school committee member. In it I expressed my discontent with how the process was ignored and the public was not given a voice in the matter.

JR: I recommend that everybody repost or share the e-mail addresses on their FB page with a note to ask their friends to contact SC members and let them know this is not acceptable.

KK: I am just shocked.

JK: So the job is just a gift to be handed out? I thought that it was a JOB and should have a pool of talented people to choose the best of. Amazing how 90% of the things that happen in RI are backwards.

MF: That we EVEN have to write a letter or discuss this issue and many issues in Cranston is not kind of pissing me off but it really is!! Who just FALLS into a job especially in this day? We all have to work hard and prove our qualifications. This is so very disrespectful and it needs to stop. We pay A LOT of taxes in Cranston and we damn well deserve better!

EG: Aren't there rules/laws in place that dictate what is supposed to happen? Other cities don't just happily form search committees and interview many candidates out of the goodness of their hearts—they are following rules that have been created to keep things transparent. Just wondering if anyone can weigh in on what is or isn't in place in Cranston.

TK: In my opinion a prerequisite to be a superintendent of a school district should be that the candidate has a PhD.

CRT: It is absolutely ridiculous that a school committee with very little hands on knowledge or experience in education holds such power.

RP: Just shows that this school committee is ok with the lack of vision for the Cranston schools. At least look elsewhere.

MH: As I said on another post sounds like a backroom deal and I agree I pay a LOT of taxes.

AD: I know I may have missed this somewhere above… But is there any chance this is an INTERIM appointment?

KK: No Anne, 100 percent not interim.

AD: Just emailed all committee members; this is just appalling…

DF: Surprised? No. Disappointed? Yes. Interestingly to note too is that the SC's Policy has been removed from the web site. "The Cranston School Committee Policy Manual is in the process of being updated."

KFD: Only in Rhode Island. I am highly disappointed in this decision…that's all I'm going to say.

PK: This has everything to do with the process not the people.

MH: We are not saying she is not qualified. It's the fact they just went ahead and promoted her without any input from parents or a search. How do we know there might not have been a local administrator more qualified? We don't because no one looked.

PK: For example, they didn't simply promote the next guy in line the last 2 police chiefs. Agree or disagree, there was a process that was followed, that's all that was pointed out, not the qualifications of the lone candidate. There was no public process in the hiring.

NH: She could be, hands down, the most qualified person for the position. It's irrelevant. The most qualified person should have been hired AFTER a proper search and interview process was done.

I'm neither a contributor to BASICS nor am I an advocate of social media. However, I am forced to agree with the last three posts especially. Regardless of a person's credentials or standing in the community, there should be a defined protocol in place for fill-ing any vacancy, especially a promotional position atop a hierar-chy. When all is said and done and the proper candidate search and screening has been performed, if the committee's choice candidate is the last man or woman standing, so be it. All the power to him or her! Congratulations. Clearly however, that is not what happened in 2015. If the taxpayers, most notably the passionate contributors to BASICS, wanted to force the issue, they could insist that upon the expiration of the superintendent's next contract, the position must be properly posted. The parents of children in the school system have shown they have the necessary influence to put the pressure on polit-ical dignitaries to make things happen.

I remember April of 2015 all too well. While the superinten-dent elect was jubilantly preparing for her uncontested coronation, I walked into my parents' house to find my mother dead on the floor. I subsequently had to go to the nursing home in which my father resided to tell him that the woman he had been married to for for-ty-eight years was gone. Whatever the correct words may have been for an occasion like that, I'm not sure I recited them. I do know, how-ever, it was the most difficult day of my life and far more distressing than anything the superintendent can invoke against me.

Upon returning to school from bereavement, I called the man who was in the same position as I was at the crosstown high school. In regard to the appointment of the new superintendent, I said to him, "We're in trouble." He did not understand my reasoning. I told him that, having already been on the wrong side of the desk with this woman and with her now being in a position to strike people down with impunity, it was problematic. My counterpart felt that although my appraisal of the new superintendent's potential had merit, he and I would be "insulated." From that point on, the only contact I had with the superintendent was at school events and award ceremonies, and on those occasions she was not willing to offer me any more than a perfunctory hello. I was informed by Principal Boober that she was quite concerned about two contracts I had negotiated on behalf of the school for photography and yearbook publishing. Apparently, the principal of the other high school had taken the position that it was unfair that his school was not receiving the same considerations for his school's photography and yearbook publishing. The superintendent intended to break the two contracts I had consummated. I was quite vocal in my belief that such action would be totally unjust. Both contracts were serving the school and the students very well. Principal Boober had signed off on both of them. I didn't think it was fair for my school to be penalized because my counterpart at the other high school wasn't diligent enough to secure quality agreements for their school. In the end, the business office announced that both of my contracts would be honored. Although I am no longer present to oversee them, both contracts should remain in place until June of 2021.

All of the graduations, award ceremonies, and special events I attended included "platform guests" who were invited to be on stage. I always found it fascinating that the bulk of the people to be exalted with that honor were the people who had the least impact on students. They didn't teach any classes. They didn't write any college recommendations. They did not advise any extracurricular activities. Nevertheless, they were showcased as the true icons of the school district. Once in twenty-four years, I was invited to be a platform guest with a speaking part. On that occasion, Principal Boober inexplicably thought it would be "sentimental" to present the superintendent with our sixtieth anniversary yearbook upon calling her to the podium. I knew the woman could care less about the yearbook, didn't want it, and was not going to acknowledge the effort that went into it or the exceptional quality of the finished project. I did not expect her to say, however, as she was handed the yearbook, "Oh yeah, the yearbook I'm not in." I heard that sitting on stage, and many others did as well. When it was my turn to speak, coincidentally, "yearbook" was in the presentation and poem I was reciting. I could have paused, in front of three thousand guests, and said, "And by the way, the superintendent is in the yearbook, page 6 to be exact." In addition to remarkable self-control, the main reason I did not do that was because we were all present to honor our graduates. We were there to pay tribute to the students, not the superintendent.

Chapter 8 will thoroughly document what happened to me in March, April, and May of 2019. On June 10 of that year, at 11:53 a.m., I received a call from the executive director of human resources telling me that "the superintendent is invoking an involuntary transfer upon you." I subsequently received the following letter by e-mail:

> June 10, 2019
> Dear Anthony,
>
> It has come to my attention that your position will not exist, as it is and/or where it is, for the 2018–2019 school year. Therefore, it is imperative that you are in attendance at the Teacher Assignment to be held on Tuesday June 11, 2019, at the Cranston West Auditorium at 3:30 PM. If you cannot attend, you must notify, in writing, the name of a proxy who will be in attendance for you.
>
> There will be high school positions at these meetings from which you must choose a position for the next year. If this is not clear in any way, please give me a call at Human Resources.
>
> Very truly yours,
> XXXXXXXXXX
> Executive Director of Human Resources

First, I do not like the use of "Dear" within the salutation. That polite term is generally included to show respect and benevolence. The senders do not possess those qualities. They are ruthless. Second, the letter states that my position would cease to exist; yet two days later, the position was posted and applicants solicited. Third, the year is incorrect. One would not be receiving a letter on June 10, 2019, pertaining to the subsequent 2018–2019 school year. Next, I'm directed to attend an event the very next day but was previously told on the phone I was not allowed to attend because I was on leave. Furthermore, the letter specifically states I was restricted to a high school position when there were two full-time middle school positions posted. I was told I was not allowed to pick those and could only teach at the crosstown high school or the charter school.

It could not have been more obvious that the aforementioned letter was thrown together very haphazardly without specific attention to the wording. They specifically waited until the day before the teacher assignment process to notify me of their decision, therefore depriving me of an adequate opportunity to consult with my personal attorney or the union regarding a possible response or request to go to arbitration. The teachers' contract specifically states that if an involuntary transfer must occur outside of the normal protocol, it should be for "compelling" reasons that the school administration will document and explain to the teachers' union and the individual. "Compelling" is not one of the adjectives I would use to describe the letter I received, and the personnel director was not willing to tell me over the phone what the rationale was for the superintendent's decision or why I was banned from teaching at any of the district's four middle schools. After receiving the decision and the letter, I was not contacted by a union representative regarding a potential response. My last contact with anyone union related was three weeks prior when the attorney representing the union called me to tell me I was being placed on leave for the rest of the school year. Perhaps if I was more union entrenched or a member of the political roundtable, the outcome would have been different. I am neither one of those things, however. I am an educator.

5. The Leadership Challenge

For what is a man, what has he got?
If not himself, then he has not.
To say the things he truly feels,
and not the words of one who kneels.

For anyone currently in a leadership capacity or anyone considering advancement to such a position, Rudolph Giuliani's 2002 bestseller *Leadership* is a must-read. Giuliani discusses leadership as a privilege which comes with many responsibilities. Whether dealing with breakthroughs, setbacks, or the complicated issues that characterize the standard workday, Giuliani advises preparation, reflection, accountability, and the communication of strong but flexible ideas as strategies that will bring out the best in people and pave the way for a department or organization to accomplish great things. Most employees reach a point in their careers when they feel they are ready for advancement. However, a promotional position is not suitable for every employee. I reached a point in my career when I was certain I would evolve into an effective leader.

Quite often, the people who take the greatest pride in their vocation are the ones influenced by people they profoundly admire. In any facet of life, the presence of mentors and people we look up to is a key component of self-improvement. Early in my career, I found myself emulating the values and ideals of two iconic individuals whose approach to teaching motivated me to be the best I could be.

I was a junior high school student when I gained my first exposure to Mr. William K. Waters. He was a member of the social studies department of the school I was attending. Unfortunately, I did not possess the class rank necessary to be in any of the classes Mr. Waters was teaching. However, I quickly gained knowledge of the reputation and standing he held in the building. Almost on a daily basis, my classmates in homeroom spoke of how fun and exciting his class was, as well as his passion for teaching social studies. In addition, Mr. Waters was the student council advisor; and in that role, he was actively involved with many of the school's assemblies and promotions. He later became yearbook advisor, and it is no exaggeration that no teacher could have been more absorbed in a school and its programs than William K. Waters. Though I never had the privilege of being taught by Mr. Waters as a student, I later gained the honor of being mentored by him as a member of his department.

William "Bill" Waters was the first department chairperson I worked under contractually. I was able to obtain a half-year position in 1993 and a .4 position for the entire 1994–1995 academic year. Though I knew neither position was permanent, I used them to establish a foundation for the acceleration of my career. Bill Waters, as my immediate supervisor, most certainly contributed to the fulfillment of that objective. Bill Waters was the most supportive person I ever worked under. In addition to his knowledge and expertise, there was benevolence about the man that made him a welcome presence in one's day. He had an office directly behind his classroom where he would enjoy his midday chicken soup. Many times I was invited to sit with him, and we conversed on many topics from the professional to the personal. Bill was very intent on promoting a positive work environment. He believed that if people were working together for 180 days, someone needed to step forward and foster an aura of collegiality. He took it upon himself to be that person. I adopted from him the practice of providing refreshments at department meetings. The effort to brighten an afternoon was very much appreciated by those in attendance. It's an example of the little things that can be done to show people they are valued. In a workplace, one can survive if not liked and possibly still be successful. The inability to gain the respect of others is a death sentence. William K. Waters was liked and respected by students and faculty alike. Though he passed away less than five years after his retirement, I will always cherish the opportunity I had to learn from him.

I enjoyed being a junior high school teacher very much. To those young and highly impressionable children, we were gods, and it was beyond exhilarating to be in a position to make that kind of an impact. Gaining such exaltation from students does not reveal itself as much from the high school population. Though I would have been thrilled to remain in the junior high school, the municipal logistics, especially those that pertained to a young teacher, delivered me to the high school on the other side of the city. Upon arrival, I was assigned to the department of Mrs. Sally L. Hannaway, one of the most unique individuals I've met in thirty-one years in education.

Anyone who dedicates thirty-six years of their life to one program certainly has my respect and admiration. Though she possessed a persona and managerial approach very much different from Mr. Waters, I embraced the challenge of joining her department. It was not the most pleasant of transitions. In addition to not being impressed easily, Mrs. Hannaway was not sanguine on the potential of newcomers she had no experience with, or did not personally interview, to be successful. Fortunately, Bill Waters's prognostication that I would grow on Mrs. Hannaway was correct. After an intense and sometimes turbulent inaugural period, I gained her respect while simultaneously becoming more comfortable with her leadership style.

Before I arrived at Cranston High School West in September of 1995, I had completed my graduate degree and worked within a variety of different teaching forums and assignments for five years. I was skillful and resourceful and had an idealistic energy within me often exhibited by young teachers. It was from Mrs. Hannaway, however, that I learned the true meaning and value of being an educator. During my first three years at Cranston West, I spent a lot of time with Mrs. Hannaway. Shadowing her, observing her teaching, and listening intently as she discussed the intricacies of the teaching profession taught me to love my job. I learned that if one approaches their teaching tasks with passion, dedication, and selflessness, educating young adults could be the greatest of vocations. I admired Mrs. Hannaway's willingness to reject progressive initiatives she did not feel were in the best interest of the students. Among the most valuable things I gained from her was an awareness and understanding of the hypocrisies that permeate a school, interfere with instruction, and potentially disrupt one's career.

Some of the people in the building who did not know Sally Hannaway as well looked upon her as a cantankerous sort. She was an advocate of strict policy enforcement for both students and teachers; and it was not uncommon for a staff member, myself included, to have a run-in with Sally on their resume. Prior to first period bell, she would blow a loud whistle to prompt students into the classrooms. Since the same rules applied to adults, she repeated the ritual at open house. "Let's go, folks. I want everybody in the rooms!" It was hilarious. She did have a soft spot however. I recall an occasion when we were both on cafeteria hall duty and an intellectually disabled student made her way by. The student inquired about the vibrant red attire Mrs. Hannaway was wearing. A woman who was looked upon as tempestuous by some was speaking to the student not as a corridor duty teacher, but as if the student was her granddaughter. Listening to her explain to the young female how wearing red has been symbolic in history was among the most touching things I witnessed at that school. She was a strong and tough person with a soft heart, which I believe are two of the most important qualities for being an effective leader. Mrs. Hannaway taught well into her seventies and maintained one of the best attendance records on the staff. When she decided to end her career in 2010 and I was fortunate enough to be her successor, she left me a wonderful congratulatory voice mail that I kept for nine years before it was inadvertently erased. Whatever remaining roads I may travel, I will always consider Sally L. Hannaway a positive influence. She empowered me and put me in a position to have a fruitful career.

Many of my students doubt my assertion that there are advantages to aging. Though it would be refreshing to regain youth and vitality, life experience and extended professional service time serve one well. Those qualities I brought to the position when I gained advancement in 2010. Unlike many building-level administrators who exited the classroom after minimal service time, I had twenty years of classroom experience when I became department chairperson. Though that experience heightened both my confidence and understanding of my teachers' needs, appointment to the position brought with it some very definitive challenges.

A department chairperson in my district is in the same bargaining membership as the teachers they are supervising. In that position, I could give directives, facilitate, mentor, and suggest; but I could not reprimand. I was never looking to be punitive with anyone, but on any staff there are circumstances in which a department member is in violation of school and/or district policy. I was limited to "discussing" the matter with the individual. More times than not, the situation went unresolved because the individual involved knew that, unless the matter made its way to building—or district-level administration, they were not obligated to change their behavior. Moreover, as a liaison between building administration and my department members, I often had to deliver information that was unwelcomed. Very often, a new initiative would come forward at a leadership team meeting, and I would be required to communicate it to my department members. If someone decided they didn't agree with it or were simply not going to comply with it, there was not much I could do.

I have no hesitancy admitting that, especially during my first two years in the position, I made mistakes. I had a lengthy agenda composed for my very first department meeting. The first item was a tribute to my predecessor, Mrs. Hannaway. I felt she deserved a few words to be recognized for her service to the school. Although that was totally appropriate, I failed to realize that although Mrs. Hannaway taught for thirty-six years and was department chairperson for twenty-one of those years, she was not correct about everything. It was a mistake to try to emulate her persona and her position on building issues. As I reflect upon that time, I know I was attentive to the fact that in the fifty-two-year history of the school, I was only the fourth person to be social studies department chairperson. I wanted to serve the school well, but also serve Mrs. Hannaway well. In doing so, I failed to take into consideration the importance of being my own man and to establish a culture that reflected Anthony, not Sally.

One question I struggled with from my appointment to my final day in the position was why people didn't see things the way

I did. To me, there are some very simple and obvious things that should be happening on every teaching faculty. People should be on time. There is no excuse for people to be habitually late. School began at seven thirty-seven. Teachers were required to be at their first period assignment for seven thirty. One of the many oddities of the building logistics was the allowance of students in the corridors prior to the mandated report time for teachers. Consequently, there were many students in the hallways and congregating outside of locked class-rooms without adequate adult supervision. To make matters worse, many teachers did not arrive until after the seven thirty-seven bell, increasing the possibility of a problem. There are additional issues associated with adults not being punctual. It does not set a very good example for the students. If a teacher is not on time, why should his or her students report on time? Moreover, I never understood how someone could arrive two minutes before a class was scheduled to begin, take off their coat, and instantaneously decide what they were doing on that particular school day. I absolutely have to be in the building with a minimal thirty minutes before my first class. I find that time is especially useful to not only capture a vision of how I would like the day to evolve, but being in the building early also pre-pares one for the unexpected. I have worked with many people who did not see punctuality as an important value.

There may be some districts that allow teachers to carry over unused sick days to the subsequent school year. In my district, that has never been an option. Therefore, teachers adopt the "use them or lose them" philosophy. I have never been a proponent of that practice. Of course, if one is ill or has an emergency in the family, sick days are contractually allotted for one's judicious use. Especially during my time as department chairperson, I did not appreciate people maxing out their sick days simply because they thought they were entitled to them. I did not appreciate people taking sick days to get caught up on their grading or because they attended the Sunday evening Patriots game and could not answer the bell the following morning. In the department I led, I had teachers with very pristine attendance. I also had teachers who clearly pinpointed specific days on the calen-dar on which they felt it was advantageous to take a day off. I led by example. I could not ask people on day 1 to be conscientious about their attendance if my absenteeism was excessive. Before my mother was stricken with cancer, I went twenty straight years without taking a sick day or a personal day. Therefore, I think it is safe to say I practiced what I preached.

Teaching is a professional vocation. Therefore, one should be dressed professionally. Though most school districts do not require a dress code for teachers, it should be self-evident that the way one dresses sends a clear message to students how one feels about what they do. Granted, on days with inclement weather or out-of-the-ordinary festivities taking place in the school, I may have opted for comfort over style. However, the majority of the time, I have been a jacket and tie man. I consider myself an impactful educator and choose to look like a professional, not a farmer.

Referred to in chapter 2, Abraham Maslow taught that a person's need for physical comfort and security needed to be established as a preface for achievement. The classrooms that teachers maintain become important instruments of that objective. Not every teacher can have their own classroom, but the ones who do should be striving to establish the best possible environment for learning. The classroom is more than just the place where instruction takes place. It should be a learning laboratory with décor and adornment that is stimulating and makes the subject being taught come alive. I asked all of my teachers to have their classrooms prepared for opening day, especially teachers of freshmen who needed that extra stimulation as they transitioned from the middle school. Unfortunately, many classrooms are Spartan due to lack of regard for environment or burdened by unnecessary clutter. I had one teacher in my department who hoarded everything she could get her hands on during the twenty years she was on the job. Her classroom resembled a defunct Ocean State Job Lot. Repeatedly, she was asked to clean it up, but did not do so. I felt strongly enough about the situation that I suggested that if she was not willing to keep the room tidy, it should be taken away from her and given to a teacher who was floating and had not had the opportunity to have their own domain. In yet another example of how my authority was limited, I was told I could not take the room away from her because it would become a union issue. The teacher in question was chronically late, struggled to effectively facilitate learning, and was observed asking if all of the nonperishables collected for a charity food drive were needed. She wanted to take some things home if they were not all being donated. Nevertheless, that teacher is still in the building and I am not.

At the secondary level, department chairpersons should schedule the classes being taught. They are the content specialists and have the necessary knowledge of their personnel to make informed decisions as to what can best serve the needs of the students. I spent a lot of time on department scheduling and treated the responsibility very seriously. I tried to assign people where they could do the most good. In select cases, I was obligated to keep people away from where they could do the most damage. I always considered myself fair with scheduling however and never took opportunities to "dump on someone." There were parameters in place that called for a full-time teacher to have no more than two subjects and three preps as an assignment. I tried to assign fewer than three preps, and if I had to schedule outside of the contractual parameters, I discussed it with the teacher first and gained his or her consent. I also tried to make sure no one was doing something completely out of their comfort zone and they had at least one class they could embrace and gain enrichment of their own. Some classes are considered wealth; some are considered sorrow. I tried to spread the wealth and sorrow as evenly as possible. If I had to ask someone to teach an inclusion group, I balanced it off with an honors class. It is bordering on impossible to please everyone. If one has twelve department members, one could easily have twelve different personalities to manage. I feel my performance in that aspect of the leadership position I held was credible.

In the 1980s, a Nebraska cardiologist who was performing an extensive study on the effects of stress coined the phrase "don't sweat the small stuff." The purpose of that advice is to encourage someone not to worry about things that are not important. If I'm making hot dogs for lunch and I discover I have no mustard in my refrigerator, I will not lose sleep over that. I will simply substitute relish or ketchup. However, if I'm in a leadership position, I do sweat the small stuff

83

because I do not want even a minor discrepancy to evolve into a major problem. There were many occasions when I was compelled to have an unpleasant discourse with a department member in an effort to prevent them from being subject to reprimand.

Positive Behavioral Interventions and Supports (PBIS) aims to improve the behavior of students by promoting a positive and safe environment for everyone. In 2017, my school, and specifically one administrator who was totally enamored with the concept, adopted the program. The program provided each teacher with an account that allowed them to assign "points" for admirable things students showcased. If one of my students contributed time to tutor another student who was struggling, I could assign points for the student's good will. The points could later be redeemed for gift cards or other merchandise. Administration decided to expand the parameters of the program. The assistant principals were assigning points for students who cut fewer classes than usual, reported to class five minutes late instead of ten, and remembered to bring something to write with. Students were being compensated because they did what was required or close to what was required. Like so many other initiatives that came forward, it bore no resemblance to the real world. If implemented properly, the concept has some merit, especially in the elementary and middle schools where social development begins and escalates. I and many of my colleagues did not feel PBIS was meritorious in the high school, especially the way in which administration was manipulating the mission of the program.

Though we were strongly encouraged to use PBIS, it was not required. I used it modestly. If I observed one of my students did something particularly humanitarian, I did go in and assign points. I did not assign points to students who pushed their chairs in upon leaving the cafeteria. One teacher in my department detested the initiative to the point in which he brought forth a sardonic response. He is a very good teacher. He has vast knowledge of his subject, and he is well liked by his students. One thing I often spoke to him about, however, was his inability to stop his disdain from coming to the forefront because of what he felt was a corrupt system. As I walked into his classroom one day, I saw Professional Bunk Indemnity

System in large letters on the chalkboard. It was an obvious mockery of the program the school had implemented. The teacher returned to the room after heating up his lunch in a microwave to find I had erased the phrase from the board. In speaking to him about it later, I told him it was made clear he was not obligated to employ the program if he did not want to. On that basis, there was nothing to be gained by ridiculing it publicly. Furthermore, I reminded him that everything we say and do in front of twenty-six students can easily be repeated at twenty-six dinner tables later in the evening. The teacher was clearly scoffing a school initiative. If a parent took issue with that and brought it to the attention of one of the higher-ups, I felt it would be difficult to defend. I respectfully asked the teacher to consider that. He did not contest my position. In fact, he thanked me for looking out for him.

The main role of a department chairperson is to promote the professional growth of those within his or her department. They do so much more however, including putting out fires. There were countless occasions in which my leadership and intervention was instrumental in preventing someone from incurring a serious reprimand. I had a teacher who was not following district protocol regarding grading. It was not an oversight on her part. It was an intentional disregard of required policy. Consequently, I received a large number of parental "concerns" related to the way in which the teacher was both establishing grades and reporting grades. I had an extended professional relationship with the teacher dating back to a previous school. I liked and respected her very much. However, I had to remind her that I could not successfully defend a circumstance in which a teacher was not in compliance with district policy. There will always be occasions when we find ourselves ideologically opposed to practices and initiatives. That does not however give us the autonomy to make our own rules.

Another teacher in the department would often incorporate profanity into her instructional time. Though I trained myself long ago not to be surprised by anything I see or hear in the public schools, I was admittedly stunned when, standing in her doorway, I observed her turn to a student and say, "I'm going to expletive slap you." It was brought to my attention on a different day that the same teacher, as part of an inexplicable diatribe against the principal, told a class, "He can eat his anus" (anus substituted here for a different term). I found it particularly vexing that she felt there was something to be gained by using vulgarity when engaging with students. She is a very good teacher. She is a major academic and extracurricular contributor and is very well liked by her students. She simply does not need to use obscenities to be an impactful educator. It was not an easy conversation to initiate; but I told her I did not want her to use profanity and, in general, she be attentive to the possibility of a parent calling me, administration, or perhaps even the superintendent's office. I hope she has heeded my advice. A teacher's use of profanity with students cannot be defended. If I was removed from the building for telling a student she was acting unladylike, she could certainly face disciplinary action for telling a class the principal should consume the opening at the opposite end of his digestive tract.

Overall, I had a very fine department of dedicated professionals. They were faithful to department duties and made a conscientious effort to bring forth their best teaching practices for the benefit of the students. When I conducted my department meetings, they listened attentively and respected my position on the issues I brought forth. The $120 spread of food I provided for each meeting most likely didn't hurt department climate. Nevertheless, there were some contentious moments. When I pointed out to a male teacher that he had been late seventy-four times throughout the course of the year, he actually had a defense for it. He held a different interpretation of the expectation that teachers were to be at their first period assignment no later than seven thirty. He was adamant that if he was walking through the teachers' parking lot at seven thirty or even driving onto the campus at that time, he should be deemed punctual. In the grand scheme of things, that was a minor disagreement compared to a vicious episode one teacher went out of his way to generate.

Until his departure in 2014, I had a colleague in my department who was the poster boy for work to rule. If he had the slightest inclination that he was going to be asked to do something more than what was contractually required, he was on the phone to the union president at his earliest convenience. He was clearly irked when I was appointed department chairperson. A very good friend of his was a finalist for the position and had long been expected to obtain the position. They both had visions of sugar plums and the establishment of a good ole boys network in which they would turn the social studies wing into their own personal playground. Much to his chagrin, his buddy was outscored during both rounds of interviews. He quickly ascertained that his best option was to become a disruptive obstructionist who would recruit members of the department to adopt his way of thinking, the belief that no one, at any time, should do anything more than they were contractually required to do.

As the 2011–2012 academic year was nearing conclusion, Principal Knowlton decided to forego a June faculty meeting. In lieu of that meeting, he communicated to us that we could bring our departments together if we saw the need to do so. He then sent an e-mail to the entire faculty specifically informing teachers that their department chairs might request that teachers come together. With final exams about to begin, I deemed it necessary to bring my department together. On a Sunday night, I sent out an e-mail to my entire department communicating my desire to meet on Monday afternoon to "reiterate final exam protocol and discuss end-of-the-year business." Specifically, I needed twenty minutes to go over a few details and distribute the exams I was nice enough to copy and collate for them. I received no e-mail in return from any department member citing opposition to having a meeting. During the Monday school day, I crossed paths with several department members. On the chance they had not read their e-mail, I reiterated to each of them my desire to have an abbreviated meeting. None of them shared with me any opposition to having a meeting; nor did they indicate that doing so was an imposition in any way, shape, or form. I therefore ended the school day at 2:00 p.m. expecting a pretty routine afternoon.

Shortly after the 2:00 p.m. dismissal, as I was finishing assisting a student with an assignment and was preparing to proceed to the meeting, the obstructionist department member appeared in my office doorway. He did not ask me to step outside to speak with him. He did not respectfully ask the two students who were in my office at the time to step out so he could speak with me. Instead, he stated sternly, "NO MEETING THIS AFTERNOON." After a brief exchange, the obstructionist went into the adjacent classroom to tell another department member she did not have to attend the meeting. He obviously had been making the rounds encouraging department members to disregard the request. Not expecting anyone to have reported to the meeting, I instead went down to Principal Knowlton's office to inform him of the developments. After that conversation, the main office secretary summoned all social studies teachers still in the building to report to our usual meeting room. I then returned to that room, only to find the obstructionist waiting in the doorway for me. He emphatically told me I could not have a meeting. I told him I was not going to argue with him, and if he was going to continue to take issue with me, he could go downstairs and speak to Mr. Knowlton. At that point, he left and did not return. I did subsequently hold a brief meeting, but it was expectedly and unnecessarily cold due to the way in which the obstructionist raised the ire against me.

It was among the most egregious episodes I experienced during the twenty-four years I was in that school. To this day, I maintain my position that the behavior of the instigating teacher was reprehensible. Principal Knowlton agreed with me, and he drafted a letter of reprimand against the obstructionist and forwarded it to the personnel office. What was especially disquieting about the entire episode was that the department members at that time had full knowledge that, for two consecutive years, I had donated my full chairperson's stipend toward additional books and supplies, awards to sufficiently recognize students at both junior and senior honors nights, and catering to provide refreshments at department meetings. I didn't feel it was unreasonable to ask them to come together for a few extra minutes of their time. I also felt it was a particularly sad testament that some of those same people had reserved their greatest passion and fervor for the teachers' union, instead of the students who so much needed their guidance and support.

The first of the previous two teachers discussed arrived at Cranston West by way of the jamboree, now referred to as the teacher assignment process. It is an event in which teachers can bid on positions district-wide they are certified for by way of seniority. A department chairperson has no control over who may join their staff or depart by way of the teacher assignment process. When the obstructionist left my department to take an administrative position in another district, it led to the only occasion I had in nine years to interview a prospective replacement. An interview session is very valuable. It becomes important to screen the applicants in a way that provides a true indication of who will represent the best investment in the school and its students. The process of identifying who that person will be is exciting, but critical. The best person for the position must be chosen.

I was informed by the principal at that time, Theodore Boober, that fifty-three persons had declared an interest in the position by submitting letters of intent to the personnel office. He also shared with me his intention to interview only seven of those candidates. I was not invited to contribute to the decision of which seven would be chosen, nor was I provided with the opportunity to examine the portfolios of the candidates. I was however provided with the names of the seven interviewees. Fortunately, included on the list was the person I felt would be best for the position. She was a young woman who had completed long-term substitute assignments at the two main high schools and had quickly developed a reputation of being passionate, conscientious, and someone who would work diligently to make a powerful impact on the students she would be assigned to.

Principal Boober had a different perspective. He quickly brought to my attention a woman who had worked in another district. I had never heard of her, and without the opportunity to examine the portfolios of the applicants, I would have to wait until the day of the interviews to discover why he was so euphoric about that particular candidate. Meanwhile, I contacted the program supervisor for social studies and shared with him who I felt the ideal person was to fill the vacancy. He was very familiar with my candidate of choice and agreed with me. The next question to answer was who would make up the interview committee. The program supervisor wanted a seat, and I certainly felt I was entitled to one. I would be the one to provide for, mentor, and guide the new teacher through the process of getting acculturated to the school. I wanted to have some influence in the proceedings.

I was granted a place on the interview committee. There were no surprises among the first six candidates, as they were the people who had been in and out of the school on a substitute basis and the persons expected to get primary consideration within a large pool of applicants. Before the day arrived, I gained additional information about the seventh applicant and Principal Boober's candidate of choice. Although she had never worked in the district, she was the daughter of a high-ranking member of the police department. I was not opposed to granting her an interview, but I was also thinking about the forty-six people who were not invited in. Though none of those persons had a parent who was personal friends with Principal Boober, could one or more of them have fit the mold of the ideal candidate we were looking for?

Because there were no readily available interview questions, I volunteered to compose them. We would need questions regarding the promotion of literacy and twenty-first-century skills, best teaching practices, accommodating the needs of the special education population, and communicating with parents. I also felt it was necessary to ask a question that was content based. The question would not be overly difficult to answer, but provocative to the point where it would be interesting to listen to the candidate articulate their answer. The interviews would open and close with statements from the head of the committee, Principal Boober. Each of the other members of the committee would ask a question, and the responses would be scored on a scale of one to five, with a rating of five being the best. My question was the content-based scenario that asked, "If you could spend thirty minutes with any one person in history, who would you select, and what would you choose to discuss with that person?" Principal Boober's candidate of choice struggled to generate an answer to the question. Her eventual response was "There are so many people to choose from. I don't know if I can narrow it down to one." When she walked out of the interview forum, Principal Boober said she was impressive. My immediate response to that was "Theodore, in addition to the fact that, having never worked in the system in any capacity, we don't have any viable references to gauge her teaching skill, she could not identify one person in history that was intriguing and impactful. For someone who is supposedly a certified social studies teacher, I am not particularly impressed with that."

Fortunately, when all of the scores were tabulated, the political football was intercepted. The person I knew was best for the position, and the program supervisor's candidate of choice, outscored the other interviewees by a sizeable margin and was subsequently appointed to the position. Just as I expected, my new appointee had a marvelous first year. She put forth great effort into both her teaching and getting acclimated to the building. She exhibited qualities not always observed in young teachers. I was most impressed with her ability to remain humble. Unlike many new teachers who quickly develop a delusion of grandeur once they have attained full-time employment, this young woman was always open to suggestions from me and the other veteran teachers in the department as to how to continue to improve her craft. I am very proud of her for what she has accomplished in the early years of her career. Unfortunately, budget cuts resulted in her temporarily losing her position and incurring a transfer to a less desirable position. However, she has currently regained her original position, and I know she will continue to prove to be the impactful educator we invested in in 2014.

I am no longer in a position to observe the professional growth of the aforementioned young woman or any of my other former colleagues in what was my department. Prior to the start of the subsequent school year, I thanked my former colleagues for their loyalty and support and sent them the following farewell:

Dear Friends:
    This communication is far overdue. However, I know you all understand my spring and summer did not evolve in the way in which I was hoping. To be 100% honest with all of you, I did not open your gift until recently. I knew I

would not be able to control my emotions, which even at this moment, is proving to be difficult.

Thank you so much for your generosity, and, more importantly, the sentiment behind it. I consider myself extremely privileged to have worked with all of you. We shared so much more than just curriculum and spanakopitas.

No department does it better than you do. You offer your students a terrific network of courses and provide a marvelous learning experience and atmosphere. I will miss watching you do what you do. I will miss the daily camaraderie and banter. There are things I will not miss. I do not believe we should be making deals with parents that simultaneously make the building principal look good. I do not believe students and parents should be managing the building when supposedly credentialed administrators should be carrying out that task. I certainly do not believe that a student and her mother should be able to decide that someone should no longer be a teacher, and put the necessary pressure on the superintendent to make it happen.

After much reflection, I have come to the realization that sometimes we have to let the river flow in the direction that it is meant to flow in. Unfortunately, my teaching values and beliefs no longer correlate with the direction in which Cranston West is moving. I sincerely did my best to look out for all of you. Now, my last directive to you is to please look out for yourselves, and for each other, as the toxicity level continues to escalate at an alarming rate. Hopefully, however, moving forward, we will all feel a sense of HOPE. As stated so truthfully in one of my favorite movies, "Hope is a good thing, maybe the best of things, and no good thing ever dies."

Be hopeful, my friends, and know that you forever have my respect, admiration, and gratitude.

Sincerely,
Anthony F. Loporchio

I neither regret pursuing advancement nor do I regret serving in that capacity for nine years. The opportunity for advancement is an important element of employee satisfaction, morale, and retention; and I would strongly encourage any employee to pursue a leadership position they feel they are qualified for. The chance to advance motivates one to excel and can place one in a forum where they can accomplish great things. Simultaneously, one must maintain the realization that, as fragrant as some of the facets of leadership may be, there are also aspects of it that have a defined stench.

6. Parental Guidance Insisted

So we open up a quarrel, between the present and the past.
We only sacrifice the future. It's the bitterness that lasts.
So don't yield to the fortunes, you sometimes see as fate.
It may have a new perspective, on a different day.

As I was looking over my itinerary for the day and week one early Monday morning, one of my Dominican students (Laisha) came into my classroom and most thoughtfully gave me a large batch of sancocho, a Caribbean beef stew consisting of meat, tubers, and vegetables served in a broth, with a small bowl of rice on the side. Almost simultaneously, a former student from my previous school was posting a derogatory video on the Internet calling me a disgusting creep. She claimed I tortured her as well as said and did nasty things to female students. I will introduce her more thoroughly in a subsequent chapter, but the two aforementioned students represent an amazing contrast. There are students who are the epitome of those we want to graduate. They not only are academically inclined but also exhibit a kindness, a sensitivity to other people's feelings, and an empathy far above the average adolescent. Conversely, there are students who are so absorbed in their own vanity and narcissism that they disrupt the school and violate the rights of others. The concept of decency is alien to them. The disparity derives from more than one factor. Certainly, the environment one is exposed to will be a precursor for their behavior and social interaction. However, the person one becomes is also greatly influenced by one's parental upbringing.

Becoming a mother or father is easy. It is the result of an uncomplicated biological process. Being a PARENT, on the other hand, is a totally different concept. I respect the concept of parenting very much, as those who bring children into the world have the most difficult tasks to carry out. No parents are perfect. Even the most loving, dedicated, and committed parents make mistakes. However, there is a colossal difference between being a parent who makes mistakes from a parent who is an egregiously deleterious influence on his or her child.

There is a definitive relationship between parenting styles and a child's social and emotional development. Although some parents employ their own methods to prepare their children for adulthood, most parents fit into one of four distinct models. The authoritarian parents have very defined and rigid standards for what they consider appropriate behavior. They insist on obedience and compliance. When a behavioral issue comes to the forefront, there is no room for negotiation with the authoritarian parent. Authoritarian parents tend to be unsympathetic and are not proponents of positive reinforcement. I have not encountered a large percentage of authoritarian parents during my time in the public schools.

A larger percentage of the parents of the current adolescent generation tend to be authoritative. Though the authoritative parents often have firm behavioral expectations for their children, they tend to be more encouraging and more empathetic than the authoritarian guardians. Authoritative parents exhibit the realization that, as children get older, they will make better decisions and therefore can be granted a greater level of independence than is seen in the authoritarian household. As a result, the communication between authoritative parents and their children is often very positive.

Unfortunately, the largest percentage of students I have taught have been the offspring of permissive parents. Though I can appreciate the affection permissive parents are known for, that affection often takes the place of discipline and the establishment of proper boundaries and parameters. I have found the children of permissive parents to be immature, moody, and tending to escalate problems rather than showcasing the necessary skills to deflate them. The most disquieting characteristic of the children of permissive parents is the total lack of awareness that words and actions have consequences.

Such children tend not to accept responsibility for their actions and infrequently express regret or remorse for their wrongdoing.

The last parenting style was once in the vast minority, but unfortunately is becoming more prevalent. Sometimes referred to as rejecting or neglecting, the uninvolved parents do not provide their children with adequate care, supervision, or moral guidance. Uninvolved parents place their own needs before their children's. They do not accept the necessary financial responsibility for their children and do not sufficiently monitor their children's activities, especially when the children reach the age in which they are out of the house more often. The children I have taught of such parenting have often been impulsive, aggressive, disrespectful, and totally insensitive to the rights of others. Their behavior is often a prelude for a dark and somber entry into adulthood. There may or may not be a "best" style of parenting. However, the aforementioned descriptors, most often permissive, were illustrated in a wide variety of stunning scenarios I have witnessed as a public school teacher.

The amount of contact a teacher has with parents depends on multiple factors. Having taught the bulk of my career at a school with a very affluent demographic, I readily expected to have an average of three to five communications with parents each week. At the inner city school I am presently teaching at, I have not had one parental inquiry the entire year. My colleagues at this inner city school concur that it is highly unlikely to receive more than three to five in any given year. For the two open houses at the inner city school, I welcomed a total of ten adults representing six different students for the six classes on my teaching schedule. Another factor is the specific levels one is teaching. On many occasions at the affluent school, open house was standing room only for Advanced Placement and honors classes, but the lower-level classes were sparsely attended. The parents of the comprehensive classes are the adults we need to speak to the most, but those parents tend to be the aforementioned uninvolved guardians or the ones who simply decline to take an active interest in their child's education.

Teachers are currently expected to maintain active communication with parents. The administration and guidance counselors at my present school want us to report to parents any unusual pattern, such as excessive absenteeism. I had a student one semester who did not report to a single class two months into the instructional period. The guidance counselor said it was imperative to call home and notify the parent(s) of that trend. I disagree that the responsibility to notify the parent of truancy lies with me. That's why we have truant officers, especially when the student's transcript indicates the absenteeism has gone unresolved over multiple years. I will respond to any request for parental communication within twenty-four hours, often sooner. However, I admittedly initiate contact infrequently, usually restricting those calls to behavioral concerns or what I feel is a need to clarify a miscommunication that took place. I do recall one definitive example when I did initiate communication and specifically requested the parent come in to school for a conference.

I especially enjoyed teaching ancient history when it was a component of our district's high school social studies curriculum. To supplement my instruction on Roman politics and "bread and circuses," I would show excerpts from the motion picture *Gladiator*. District policy calls for parental consent in the form of a permission slip to be obtained prior to the presentation of R-rated film material. I stated on the permission slip what my rationale was for integrating the film into my instruction. The document offered parents the choice of consenting to have their son or daughter view the video material or having their child sent to an alternative location to complete an alternative assignment. One of the parents of this class sent the permission slip back to school with his daughter, having consented by checking off the "YES" box, but also writing on the document, "This movie is trash. Perhaps I should send my daughter to the Showcase to get her education." It was definitely one of the occasions when I saw the need to initiate communication. I particularly disliked the way in which the parent expressed his opinion. He easily could have called me up and expressed any concerns he had about my use of that particular film. Instead, he wrote abrasive comments on the consent form and put it in his daughter's hands to deliver to me. In my opinion, he set a very poor example to the daughter regarding how to go about having a concern addressed. I therefore asked the guidance counselor to set up a parent conference.

It was subsequently brought to my attention that the parent was a retired high-ranking municipal bigwig. He obviously considered most everyone else a menial unworthy of respect and courtesy. He sat with his wife next to him and spoke to me in a very demeaning manner. I was not going to argue with him. A film that won Academy Awards for Best Picture, Best Actor, Best Sound Mixing, Best Visual Effects, and Best Costumes is obviously not "trash." I simply pointed out that "When one writes what you did on the permission slip, one obviously is trying to make a statement. Therefore, by all means, please tell me what it is you do not like about my teaching." The meeting was not productive, though it is notable to point out that the daughter was later removed from a prominent activity for inappropriate behavior, subsequently dropped out of school, and became pregnant shortly thereafter. Perhaps Dad should have spent less time polishing his shoes and berating teachers and more time monitoring his daughter's conduct.

Parents have a natural and rightful inclination to protect their children from harm. However, there are parents who fabricate the existence of illness or disability in their children and, as a result, cause the children to be emotionally distraught and psychologically maladjusted. The disorder is called Munchausen syndrome by proxy, and I have seen it come to the forefront on multiple occasions. I distinctly remember such a scenario with a family that had two children in the school simultaneously, a son and a daughter. The father was quite sedate and rarely contributed anything tangible to any meetings regarding either the son or daughter. The mother was quite a different persona. She took a very aggressive approach with the school district, making rigid demands and threatening lawsuits far more often than considering tact to put her children in a more favorable position. Supposedly, the son had a crippling orthopedic ailment that prevented him from attending school with any regularity. During the few instances when he was present in class, he rarely spoke or made any effort to advocate for himself. It was always Mom who was giving the directives, especially in regard to the son being granted indefinite extensions for relatively standard assignments. There was one stretch in the second half of the year that the student had been out approximately twelve to fifteen weeks. Coinciding with the final weeks of the school year, I was expected to revisit assessments that were not completed literally months earlier. Again, the student never generated any discourse regarding missing work or what was still eligible to be submitted. It was Mom who told the teachers what he would be turning in and the manner in which he would do so.

In the case of the daughter, her ailment was communicated as severe headaches. For four years, she was absent the vast majority of the school year. The mother took an even more aggressive stand with the daughter's case than she had with the older son. She insisted that tutors be provided, at school department expense, to compensate for what she felt was the daughter's inability to attend school with any regularity. At the tutorial sessions, the daughter consistently stated she wasn't feeling well and, on that basis, usually did not have the work completed that was expected on that particular day. However, she regularly wrote in her class journal how much she enjoyed going to concerts and would offer explicit details on many of the shows she attended. Apparently, the headaches dissipated every time a major popular culture celebrity was in town. One of the teachers in my department had an especially bad experience with this young woman. According to Mom, not the student, my teacher was speaking to the student in an abusive manner. The parent insisted that the teacher be brought up on charges, and it became a union matter. Again, it was the parent who lodged the complaint, not the student. The children may indeed have had the symptoms of orthopedic and neurological illness, but the behavior of the parent was projecting the suffering onto the student, with both children never exhibiting any degree of self-sufficiency.

An even more intense example of Munchausen syndrome by proxy coming to the forefront involved a mother who, unlike the previously mentioned parent, DID file multiple lawsuits against the school district. In each case, the parent argued that the school district was blatantly guilty of failing to meet the accommodations documented within the daughter's 504 and IEP plans. The consternation with this case reached the point where the entire school administration and all of the teachers involved were on edge regarding their interaction with the student and fearful of additional lawsuits being filed by the mother. What started out as accommodations became complete capitulation.

It was brought to the mother's attention that appropriate academic placement would likely result in a more successful experience for the daughter. The student's middle school and early high school transcripts showed enrollment in predominantly college preparatory classes. The mother was outraged at that suggestion and insisted, without the daughter's input, that she be placed in all Advanced Placement courses. Mom claimed that the daughter could not comprehend the language of a CP textbook. She had to have AP textbooks. In addition, the student would be issued three textbooks, one to carry to and from class, one to keep at home, and one to remain in her locker. The student would be issued a laptop computer, at school department expense, for notetaking. The student would be provided with a duplicate set of class notes to serve as a backup to the notes she supposedly would be taking with the laptop.

The parent demanded frequent staff meetings to ensure all of the accommodations were being met. Clearly, the parent's underlying motivation for the meetings was to put the staff on notice and reiterate previous threats of legal action against the school district and possibly individuals suspected of being noncompliant. Under normal circumstances, such meetings would be conducted by an administrator, usually the guidance director, or, as the position is currently designated, the assistant principal for academic affairs. On behalf of the student, but without input from the student, the parent would immediately take over the meeting. She would then frantically flick the light switch on and off to simulate the difficulty her daughter was experiencing in each class. Additional demands would be made at every meeting, and before the student completed her high school experience, there were some revisions to the IEP that I have never seen in more than thirty years in the public schools.

First, the student lost the laptop she was issued. The school department had to replace it and incur the expense of doing so. A clause was added to the IEP stating that if a teacher made contact with the student in another classroom or another part of the building, they were not to acknowledge her or draw attention to her in any way. The mother had convinced the daughter that such action would be traumatizing. Furthermore, the parent instilled anxiety upon the student regarding having to exit the building in an expeditious manner. Therefore, the final IEP required teachers to remind the student to hold on to the railing during a fire drill. The student would vehemently object to the reminder, but the teachers did not want to risk being accused of failing to comply with the IEP. Fortunately, for all staff members involved, the student did finally graduate. The teachers of the student collectively concurred it was the most anxiety-provoking case of their careers. They also had no recollection of the parent ever extending any gratitude for the multifarious accommodations that were made over the course of four years.

Staff meetings are not the only setting in which parents will express disdain for teaching practices or the way in which a school is managed. Parents will use social media quite aggressively to express their contempt for the way in which schools handle such things as IEPs and 504s, communication of important information, school safety, and even COVID-19. Perhaps the most notable forum for that discourse in my district is a social media outlet called BASICS. Benefiting All Students in Cranston Schools (BASICS) is promoted as a nonpartisan organization dedicated to finding practical solutions to the city's educational financial crisis. Their mission is to fundraise, educate, and bring attention to the issues that are facing children and their education. The forum perpetuates the belief that serious mistakes have been made in the past. According to the orchestrators of the network, every parent needs to advocate for their children so that the students do not have to pay for those mistakes for years to come. Though I agree with some of the things contributors have posted on BASICS, most notably the criticisms of the way in which central administration positions have been filled, I don't feel that feeding into an online gripe session is an overly productive way to enact change. The contributors feel they are advocating for their children on Facebook, but unfortunately they are spending too much time deferring to their children at home.

At a very young age, I was taught that, at school, the teacher was the boss. It did not matter if I didn't like the teacher, the class, or the rules. My job was to follow directions and be respectful at all times. I was a well-behaved kid. If a problem at school reached the dinner table, my parents would listen to my side of the story, but my father especially was not going to acquiesce to me and fail to hold me responsible if I was clearly in the wrong. Such accountability among the present generation of adolescents is rare. For the most part, teenagers today are overindulged and are not specifically taught that they are responsible for their actions. Their behavior is reinforced by unbridled and irresponsible use of social media and the dubious conduct of the popular culture celebrities they revere. When teaching developmental psychology, I use the following case study, which is based on a true story:

> *Mrs. Clackstein, an eleventh grade high school English teacher, calls the father of a female student in her period 1 class and tells him she has documentation that his daughter posted on Twitter that Mrs. Clackstein is actively selling heroin in the students' parking lot every day after school. Outraged at such an allegation, the father vehemently denounces the teacher and categorically says, "My daughter would never do anything like that!" The next day, the parent storms into the principal's office at 7:00 a.m., with the daughter, and demands that she is transferred out of Mrs. Clackstein's class.*

The above scenario is a classic example of what teachers are facing in this day and age, especially at an affluent school where the principal is making a daily concerted effort to be a personal hero to the parents. At no time in the above case study does the parent take the opportunity to consider his daughter may have been guilty of the allegation. He does not make the effort to communicate with the teacher or ask to see the documentation she said she had in her possession. The parent instead denounced the teacher and reaffirmed the daughter's behavior, which, by definition, fit the description of criminal libel. He then made matters worse by attempting to create an avenue for the daughter to switch classes. Unfortunately, when Mrs. Clackstein reflects on her long and illustrious career, she will inevitably remember the episode which strongly contributed to her decision to retire.

The worst episode I had that was comparable to what Mrs. Clackstein experienced took place in 2007. It started with a very timid and reserved freshman male coming into my classroom at three fifteen in the afternoon. More than an hour after dismissal, he took off his jacket and began to open his backpack. He said, "I have to show you something." I interrupted him before he did so. I told him that he was welcome to tell me whatever he wanted to; HOWEVER, "whatever it is you are about to share with me, I may be bound by law, and by ethics, to report it." I honestly thought it was a child abuse situation and that the kid was taking off his jacket to show me injuries that were inflicted upon him. I honestly had no basis to draw such a conclusion, and I was very happy I was incorrect. Instead, the student took a manila folder out from his backpack. In it were more than twenty pages of postings he and his father had printed out at home. In what was a remarkable demonstration of courage by a four-teen-year-old, the young man was responsible enough to bring to my attention that a group of my former students, who were still in the school as upperclassmen, decided to use the Internet to portray me as a child molester.

Closer examination of the materials and some investigative work showed that there were several students involved, but it was one male and one female student who were the ringleaders. While hosting a party, the male student directed the production of the materials that would be posted on the Internet. His female accomplice took the role of distributing the materials by way of her main social media account. As for their motivation, it was not academic, as both students had previously achieved an "A" in my world history honors class. The male student vehemently denied his involvement; but an associate of his told me that he was upset with me because in my previous book, which had been published less than a year earlier, his girlfriend was one of the ten students I paid tribute to, but I did not acknowledge him. The female student, with her father present, admitted to her actions. The assistant principal asked her, "Why did you do it? What is your issue with Mr. Loporchio?" She responded, "Nothing. It was just something to do." None of the students involved faced any disciplinary action because what they admitted to, or allegedly had done, took place off school grounds. The school administration took the position that they had no jurisdiction in the matter. That would not be the end of the story however.

The male student was also on my yearbook staff. As a personal favor to him, I allowed him to use the large teacher's locker outside of my classroom. When I learned of the activities he had been involved in, I revoked the privilege. Without hostility, I told him I wanted the locker emptied and vacated by the end of the week. He looked at me as if he had no idea why I was giving such a directive and challenged it. Again, without raising my voice, I repeated the directive and walked away. He then followed me and insisted on an explanation. At that point, I raised my voice several octaves and told him exactly what I thought of his child molestation campaign against me. He denied his involvement. He obviously never considered saying, "Mr. Loporchio, I messed up. I made a bad decision. I'm very sorry." Given the fact that every person in this world has had an instance when they took a left turn when they should have gone right, I honestly would have shown forgiveness if any of the students involved apologized. No such regret or remorse was ever communicated to me however.

I did not see the male student again until senior yearbook night. He came to pick up his yearbook, which he was under the impression I had purchased for him. I actually had purchased yearbooks in the past for some of my seniors as a graduation gift, but I certainly was not going to buy a yearbook for a student who tried to portray me as a child molester. The student was flabbergasted when informed he did not have a yearbook reserved for him. He was politicking the faculty chaperones to convince me to give him one, but they knew better than to approach me for that. A few minutes later, the boy's mother appeared at the event. "I'm here to pick up my son's yearbook." I told her that he had not purchased a yearbook. She responded, "You told him you were buying his yearbook." Not wanting the event to be disrupted any further, I asked the parent to step into the corridor. I shared with her my feelings on what her son had done. Even though many of the pictures that were floating around on the Internet were taken in this woman's house, she refused to acknowledge her son's involvement. She told me if I did not give her a yearbook, she would report that I slammed the door of the locker her son was using into his head.

My exact response was "Mr. Knowlton is in his office every morning no later than 7:00 a.m. Absolutely, if a teacher slammed your son's head into a locker, you have to report that."

She then replied, "Why does it have to go that far? Why can't you just give me a yearbook?"

I said, "I don't give in to extortion. If you would like to purchase one of the extra yearbooks that are available, you are more than welcome to do so." She did not accept my offer and left without further incident.

The next morning, as my first period class was concluding, I received a call from the main office secretary telling me that Mr. Knowlton wanted to see me at my earliest convenience. At that meeting, he shared with me that it was brought to his attention that there had been an incident at the previous night's yearbook distribution and I had refused to give a student a yearbook. I summarized what had transpired and reiterated that the circumstances being what they were, I was not going to buy that kid a yearbook. I then asked him about the assault allegation. With a surprised look on his face, Mr. Knowlton told me he didn't know anything about that. Obviously, the parent was hoping that the mere threat she brought forth would get me to capitulate to her demand. She knew she would not be able to move forward with the allegation without being able to substantiate it with proof. What she did do, however, was give the principal seventy dollars in cash; and I was subsequently asked to provide a yearbook for that family.

When I reflect upon that episode, it disgusts me. Not only was the parent unwilling to acknowledge that her son was not the little choir boy she proclaimed him to be; she had the audacity to accuse me of a criminal act in order to get what she wanted. It was a disgraceful exhibition, and she should have been very embarrassed. She reaffirmed her son's behavior, failed to hold him accountable for his actions, and set a very bad example in the process.

I would characterize my twenty-two-year experience as yearbook advisor as spectacular, but it did include some unpleasantries with parents. In addition to the aforementioned episode, I had a parent who took issue with me for what I felt was doing her job for her. I had an eleventh grade student in US history who was a polite and well-mannered boy, but totally lacked confidence in himself. He was uninvolved in school activities and, at times, just walked around the building aimlessly. I invited him on to the yearbook staff because I thought it would provide him the opportunity to meet some of the other staff members, work with them closely, and contribute to an important project. The activity turned out to be a very positive experience for the young man. He enjoyed contributing to the yearbook, took on an accelerated role, and developed a nice relationship with the other staff members while simultaneously working very closely with me on some of the intricacies of the project. A relative of his, an alumnus to the school and well-known personality in the community, was so appreciative that I and the yearbook activity were such a positive influence he treated me to a Boston Red Sox game and dinner in one of the stadium luxury suites. The boy's mother, however, had a different viewpoint. She felt that I had overstepped my bounds as a history teacher and yearbook advisor and called the superintendent to complain about me. Fortunately, the superintendent at that time was a former teacher of the woman, was well acquainted with her pregnancy at fifteen years old, and was well aware of her unstable persona. He referred to her by a very unflattering term and told me to forget about it. It was, however, another in a long list of very odious examples of an irresponsible parent whose actions had a deleterious impact on the child.

Throughout my career as a classroom teacher, a curriculum leader, and a yearbook advisor, I have found that the most effective way to interact with parents is actually to be very attentive to their concerns. I have always made myself available for discussion of any topic. I will make an attempt to accommodate any reasonable request. I will not, however, make deals with parents, especially the types of arrangements simply agreed upon so that the principal can look good. One of the most horrendous examples of that type of scenario involved a student who missed 167 days of school. This female student supposedly had a neurological disorder that prevented her from attending school with any frequency. Her academic records showed that the absenteeism could be traced back several years. In our school, disregarding the advice of teachers and her guidance counselors, the student insisted on being in all Advanced Placement classes. The student had an IEP which called for teachers to grant "extended time" to complete assessments. There was never any specification as to what "extended time" meant. Quite often, such plans will document a 50 percent extension for the submission of work. In other words, if a class is granted four weeks to complete a project, the student with the accommodation would be granted six weeks to submit the assignment. Without any specificity documented, the student decided to establish her own timeframe for the submission of work.

I was not the teacher of the above student, but when I have had to overlook similar cases, I have always been reasonable with my expectations. If I am asking a class to submit an assignment for October 1, I feel it is reasonable for a student who has been out or is afflicted with an illness to provide me with the work by November 1, maybe even somewhat after that. In this case, the student decided it was reasonable to submit fall work, for an AP class, in June. She delivered to the teacher, on the second to last day of school, a large box containing various assignments she had not turned in dating back to October. The teacher considered what she was being asked to do to be completely unrealistic and unfair to the other enrollees. In discussion with the teacher, I told her it was her call on what she felt she could accept and not accept. If she wanted to accept all of the work, I would support that decision. If she decided not to accept any of the work, I would back her up if that decision was challenged.

My teacher decided that, even though it was two days before the end of school and final exams had already taken place in most classes, she would accept the work that had been done for the final marking period, retroactive to early April. As her immediate supervisor, I felt that was reasonable, fair to the other enrollees, and certainly not a violation of any IEP or 504 that was in place. Complicating this case was the insistence by the student and her mother that not only all of the work be accepted but also that the grade for the course should be an "A." Apparently such deals had already been consummated in three other subjects, and it now all came down to social studies for the family to hit the grand slam they were looking for.

The mother of the student employed an intimidating demeanor and clearly took advantage of the fact that the other three departments she was negotiating grades with were all led by people who were new to their positions. One was out of the building on maternity leave. The other two had their inexperience used against them and capitulated easily. The student and her mother made one final attempt at an "A" in US history. I received a call from the guidance counselor asking me to call the parent. When I got back to the counselor, she told me the parent was actually in the building and everyone was prepared to come right up to my office to discuss the situation. For almost ninety minutes, I listened to the parent and student rationalize why having completed less than 50 percent of the required work for an Advanced Placement class, an "A" should be assigned as the final grade. I reiterated that it was my teacher's call as to how much work she was willing to put a grade on during the last week of school, when her time should have been restricted to grading final exams. I also took the opportunity to show the student, the mother, and the guidance counselor e-mail transcripts from the teacher to the student reminding her about missing work and respectfully asking the student when the work could be expected. There were answers to the teacher's inquiries from the student promising the work was "on its way." In summary, the student was absent 167 of the 179 instructional days. She was tardy on eight occasions and dismissed early on four others. She was not in school for an entire instructional day once. Somehow, all of that translated into a B+, A–, and an A in Spanish, Math, and English, respectively.

When all was said and done, the student had an F—in US history on her transcript with all of the other grades that had been negotiated. Truthfully, neither I nor my teacher took any satisfaction with the student failing the course. It was a simple matter of academic integrity and making a decision that was fair to everyone involved. Of course, the decision was not popular with administration. My teacher and, to a greater extent, I as department chairperson were looked upon as inflexible. Here's a brief news bulletin for administration. Assigning a student the grade of "A" for a course in which she completed less than 50 percent of the work does not make one flexible. It makes one an imbecile.

Why is it that we mostly only hear from the parents who have an axe to grind? Just once, I would feel refreshed to receive an e-mail or phone call from a parent commending me for not giving tests on Mondays. It would be stimulating if a parent acknowledged me for understanding that students are under a lot of pressure and that by keeping the workload reasonable and establishing flexible timeframes to complete assessments, I am maintaining a stress-free classroom. Is it unreasonable for me to believe that there could be a parent who considers the more than thirty-four thousand dollars I have spent on candy, awards, and prizes throughout my career to be admirable generosity?

This chapter will close with two final examples of the permissive parenting that has dominated the text. Overall, the students' fixation on their mobile devices is certainly among the biggest obstacles to classroom instruction. Some students are more responsive and respectful about the visibility of the cell phones in the classroom than others. I can recall a student who was constantly text messaging. She had a seat closer to the front, and even when I would direct subtle body language in her direction to prompt her to put the phone away, she would keep right on texting. She either didn't care that she was being disrespectful while I was teaching, or she thought Stevie Wonder was teaching the class and could not see what she was doing.

At open house, her mother received a phone call during my presentation. Not only did she take the call; she carried on a conversation while I was addressing the other parents. It became clear at that point that the daughter's inability to understand that what she was doing was wrong stemmed from the parent's own lack of etiquette. Interestingly, that was also the only parent who ever questioned a class participation grade I assigned a student. Mom told me the daughter should have an "A" for that component of the grade because she participated all the time. Well, if class participation means text messaging three quarters of the period, then yes, I should have given her full credit for that component of her course grade.

Finally, I had a parent who took the position that the B—her daughter was maintaining in my class did not correlate with the effort the student was putting forth. Though the student had a decent grade in the course, above average as defined in the student handbook, she was lazy. Every time a task required three steps for completion, she was only willing to complete one or two. She did not have a higher grade because she simply did not give the class the time an honors course warranted. What I found most interesting about the student, however, was something she shared with me in her class journal. She described her home and how it was completely equipped with an intercom system. If she was in her bedroom and wanted a cup of coffee, a back rub, or her toenails painted, she would use the intercom to call someone to fulfill the request. She also wrote in the journal entry that if she felt her request was not being accommodated fast enough, she would verbally reprimand the service provider.

The last two examples perfectly illustrate that parents need to provide their children with more structure and less materialism. Though I have met some wonderful parents throughout my career, I became acquainted with a larger percentage of parents who failed to understand that cell phones and intercom systems are not the best tools to put their children on the road to having a fruitful adulthood. Teachers are always being asked what they can do to give their students a better chance to succeed. That is a valid question. However, an equally legitimate question is, are teachers failing their students, or are parents failing their children?

7. East Is East and West Is Definitely West

The whispered conversations,
in overcrowded hallways.
The atmosphere is thrilling here, as always.
Feel the early morning madness.
Feel the magic in the making.
Why, everything's as if we never said goodbye.

T hough only three miles apart, the city's two main high schools are vastly different forums. Cranston (East) High School, which was built in the late nineteenth century, is now educating predominantly inner city students. In the short time I have taught there, I have found the students to be respectful and compliant to disciplinary protocol. With just a few exceptions, they speak to each other in a tolerant and courteous manner, clearly embracing the diversity that makes their school special. Passing times are remarkably quiescent. Students are not seen shoving each other into lockers, hording in the lavatories, or causing unnecessary commotion as they move from one class to another. Those things are regular occurrences at "the school on the other side of the city," as it is referred. Interestingly, Cranston East students forego surnames when speaking to teachers and address us as Mr. or Miss. They are loquacious with each other, but frustratingly sedate interacting with teachers. They say very little on the way into the classroom and next to nothing upon dismissal. There are many students who literally seem scared to speak while a lesson is being taught. In general, unlike their counterparts at Cranston West, Cranston East students do not look to draw attention to themselves or seek out extraordinary measures to do so.

The greatest distinction I have observed between the Cranston East Thunderbolt and the Cranston West Falcon is the extent in which the students are emotionally invested in their educational opportunities. The main reasons for that are unquestionably cultural. Due to socioeconomic status, a lower level of educational attainment by parents, and a language barrier, education is not a priority to a high percentage of Cranston East students. While Cranston West students are waking up to the smell of freshly baked croissants and cappuccino, Cranston East students typically arrive without a morning meal and rely on the school's breakfast program. While a Cranston West student is requesting to have his Mercedes or BMW valet parked, a Cranston East student is dropped off by school bus or is walking a considerable distance, often in inclement weather. While the Cranston West student is arguing with parents about a weekly allowance, Cranston East students as young as freshman year are working in the community in order to contribute to the household budget. While the typical Cranston West student is signing up for as many activities as possible to strengthen college applications, the typical Cranston East student must forfeit extracurricular opportunities because they have to be home promptly to take care of younger siblings. While the Cranston West Winter Ball is being attended by more than five hundred students and the girls are competing with each other to showcase the most stunning dress, the very same event is being simultaneously canceled at Cranston East because of a lack of student interest. They are indeed two very different places, but the school in which I spent twenty-four years of my professional life requires a deeper analysis.

The 1950 census recorded the population of Cranston, Rhode Island, at 55,060. The 1960 census showed a population of 66,766. An increase of almost twelve thousand people in one decade escalated concerns over the ability of the city to properly educate its school children. Recognizing the continued expansion of Cranston and the aging of the city's only high school, a good portion of the 1950s was devoted to planning the construction of a second high school. Cranston West has the distinction of being one of very few high schools built on a time plan. From the very beginning, it was never an entire entity, a complete school. With the first phase opening for classes in September of 1958, it became necessary for the school to adopt its colors and select a mascot. Those tasks were initiated by then Assistant Principal Joseph Coccia, who went from room to room with various colors of construction paper to gain input from students as to what would make the best school colors. After careful consideration, students found the combination of charcoal gray and red most to their liking. The falcon was chosen as the school mascot because students considered what they were looking to accomplish comparable to a falcon "flying high." "Falcons Flying High" is still a motto employed at the school today. Students and staff members who have been part of the Cranston West community are considered part of the Falcon family and are designated as "Forever Falcons." The current school campus rests on twenty-six acres and consists of a central classroom building, a career and technical center, a gymnasium, a business and technology building, an auditorium and music center, and an extensive athletic area.

Before September 18, 1990, I had never set foot in Cranston High School West. In fact, I was not entirely certain where in the city the school was located. My earliest memories of the school include having an apple thrown at me while on lunch duty, being karate kicked while covering a Russian class, and a group of students who, for some reason, felt the need to ridicule my surname. Given what I was exposed to during those early years, it was inconceivable that it would be the place I would teach for the bulk of my career. However, when the district made the decision to move the ninth grade to the high schools in 1995, I, along with a host of other educators who were teaching ninth grade, went with them.

The best things I have done in my life were at Cranston High School West. During the twenty-four years I was there, I was privileged to teach a large number of students who were gifted with both scholastic excellence and personal character. I enjoyed teaching my classes immensely. I am grateful for the opportunity to work with a large array of dynamic colleagues. I am proud to have gained advancement to a leadership position. I am proud to have orchestrated the effort to produce twenty-two yearbooks, thus chronicling

113

and preserving the history of the school. I honestly believe that, with a few subtle changes to managerial policy and a more credible commitment to hold students accountable for their actions, Cranston High School West could be in the same conversation with the top-ranked public high schools in Rhode Island. Unfortunately, every school has entities and circumstances that develop which interfere with teaching and learning.

Each state is required by its state constitution to provide a school system whereby children receive an education. However, education is a privilege, not an entitlement. Contrary to the position of the Rhode Island Department of Education, I have always maintained that when a student proves beyond a reasonable doubt that he or she is not willing to comply with school protocol, they forfeit their opportunity to be educated. Those who spend the majority of the school week disrupting the school, harassing their classmates and teachers, and generally making it as difficult as possible for other students to grasp what the teachers are facilitating should be expurgated. For one student fitting that description, the disruption he caused resulted in a group of teachers approaching Principal Boober and campaigning for the student's permanent dismissal. The response was "You people don't know how difficult it is to remove someone." I doubt any of those teachers said so, but the obvious reply would have been "You didn't run into any difficulty removing Anthony."

Effective teaching and learning depends on a positive school climate. Especially in a large school, it is imperative that proper discipline is maintained in order to have such a climate. That concept is not a proficiency of Cranston High School West. One should have a minimum of ten years of classroom teaching experience before advancing to building-level administration. Four of the six current administrators do not have such a background. At a leadership team meeting, Principal Boober bristled when I suggested that each administrator teach a class on an annual rotating basis in order to maintain an understanding of the pedagogical challenges the faculty faces on a daily basis. How can one support and understand the plight of the classroom teacher if their service time within that capacity is minimal? As a result, the corridors are out of control, and I myself on numerous occasions felt my safety was in jeopardy.

A good example that comes to mind was when, on my way to an administrative meeting, I took note of the vivacious but inexperienced Assistant Principal Edith Forbes attempting to deal with a group of male students loitering in the lavatory. I asked if she wanted me to go in and move them along. Her immediate response was "No, no, no, it's my job. Your job is to teach AP psychology." Being a curious man, I decided to stick around for the outcome. Mrs. Forbes repeatedly called out to the loiterers, but they would not comply with her directive. Then, one student, the obvious ringleader, shouted out, "Just let me take an expletive s——t in peace." What did Edith Forbes do at that point? She walked away with the group still in the lavatory, well after passing time. What should Edith Forbes have done at that point? She should have called the school resource officer and asked him to remove the students. At that point, if they do not comply with the police officer, arrest them for disorderly conduct. Make those miscreants talk about being arrested on social media instead of granting them the satisfaction of posting how they made a fool out of the assistant principal.

One particularly disgusting behavior that developed was students writing graffiti on bathroom walls in the form of death threats. On one occasion, I was part of a group who responded to a death threat on the second-level boys' bathroom wall targeting Principal Boober and his wife. All but one of the members of the administrative team were out of the building at that time. We immediately reported the discovery to the main office and asked for the sole administrator present, Edith Forbes, to come upstairs. Upon her arrival, she was not sure what to do. Clearly, someone needed to take photographs of the threat posted and immediately lock the lavatory. There was no need for additional students to go into that bathroom, discover the threat, and subsequently generate unfounded gossip on social media. We made those suggestions to Mrs. Forbes.

According to the Rhode Island Department of Education, "school disciplinary measures should not be used to exclude students from school or otherwise deprive them of an education. Out of school suspension should be used as a last resort in schools in order to preserve the safety of students and staff." When a student aggressively confronts a teacher, should that be considered a threat? When a student uses bullying and intimidation tactics to resolve a problem with a teacher, should that be considered a threat? When a student threatened to kill one of my department members, should that student have been removed from the school? When students are guilty of infractions that are felonies outside of the school, should they not be subjected to punitive action? Is the effort to not deprive the incorrigibles of an education in essence violating the rights of the responsible and conscientious students? Those questions came to the forefront in a series of events I witnessed in which little to no discipline was invoked.

Not all students have a wonderful high school experience. I certainly did not. Though I always did well academically, I struggled with the social aspects. My senior year was particularly unenjoyable. Nevertheless, I did not see the need to strike back against the school for not accommodating all of my needs. Unfortunately, not every twelfth grader accepts their diploma with dignity and walks away peacefully. Some seniors feel the need to leave a lasting negative imprint through vandalism, felonious acts, or what they consider "pranks." I have witnessed some notable senior pranks during my years as a high school teacher.

There was one senior class who thought it would be amusing to unleash an orchestra of crickets inside the main building. The science teachers must have taught those students well. They learned that crickets mate in late spring and will lay hundreds of eggs. The seniors decided to release the crickets in the cafeteria and kitchen area to make them more ravenous. It took a considerable amount of time to resolve the infestation. The individuals responsible were never identified and held accountable.

I can vividly recall driving onto the campus on a late May morning and seeing a giant inflatable Shrek on the roof of the main building. It was later made known that the inflatable ogre belonged to the neighborhood Burger King and was once perched atop its roof. A group of seniors removed it from Burger King's roof and put it on the roof of Cranston West as a prank. Though the stunt induced laughter from a great number of people, in reality, it was grand larceny and was not something to be celebrated. An ominous commonality between the cricket and Shrek incidents was that, in both cases, the main motivation of the seniors carrying out the pranks was their belief that they would get away with them.

During the time I served as yearbook advisor, there were many unnecessary frivolities I had to deal with brought forth by senior classes. One of the more aggravating pursuits of twelfth graders was their appetite for generating fraudulent student identification cards. While standing in line for an updated school photo, they would switch cards with each other. If Sally switched cards with Suzie, Sally's image would appear on Suzie's ID card. The many seniors who did this were not concerned about incorrect photos appearing in the yearbook because they knew their yearbook pictures had been taken off campus in a professional studio. The September sittings were solely for an updated school ID. As a result, students would have in their possession a fraudulent school ID, an official school document they then could use for multiple purposes. I considered this a serious matter. Forgery of official documents is a felony in most states. Principal Knowlton agreed with me and imposed a harsh penalty on the offenders. All of the students involved were suspended for, as Principal Knowlton classified it, sabotaging the school database. They were required to sit for new photos as well as pay the expenses of producing the new IDs. Such incidents did not reoccur during the Knowlton principalship.

When the issue resurfaced during the Boober principalship, administration did not respond nearly as seriously. Principal Boober and his next in command dismissed it as "a harmless prank that they probably Photoshopped in their bedrooms." Having directed twenty-two yearbook projects, I was eminently more qualified to conclude what the seniors had done, especially since I had documentation to support my claim. Nevertheless, no action was taken against the students, and the problem continued through my final year in the position. One of the last episodes I saw involved two female students who obviously knowingly produced fraudulent IDs, but convinced two assistant principals it was a mistake by the photographer. The first assistant principal said he discussed the incident with the students' teacher they were with at the time of the photo sittings. That teacher verified that the students did not switch cards. Not only was that teacher absent the day the pictures were taken; it was the same teacher who was sending text messages to students questioning the credentials and teaching skill of other staff members. Her credibility is dubious to say the least.

At 5:31 p.m. on a Wednesday, the second assistant principal, Edith Forbes, sent me an e-mail stating, "I guarantee that these aren't kids who would do this as a prank." Eight minutes later, at 5:39 p.m., she sent me a follow-up stating, "Just got some information. I was erroneous in my estimation of the kids." The end result was that the problem did not cease and Edith Forbes left the school after only eighteen months to pursue a promotional position in another district.

In a poorly managed school, scenarios develop that can be potentially physically threatening and violent. During the last teaching block on a Friday afternoon, I stepped into the classroom of an absent teacher in my department and found myself in a very uncomfortable situation. It was a class of thirty students with a substitute who was reading her *Harry Potter* novel instead of making an effort to manage the classroom. Students were hanging out of the emergency evacuation window. The electronic devices were rampant. Nothing academic was being done. After I sternly told the students in the back of the room to close the fire window and sit down, a student on the opposite side of the room yelled out, "Turn around and go back to where you came from! What's happening in here is none of your business." I moved closer to that student to tell him that what was going on in the room WAS my business and to tell him to put his radio, earbuds, and phone away and complete the assignment. He then responded, "Turn around and leave. The tuna fish you had for lunch is coming off your breath and stinking up the whole room." To clarify, I had chicken parmigiana for lunch that day, not tuna fish. Be that as it may, the student refused to put his devices away; and with the rest of the class literally cheering him on, I felt my best option

WAS to turn around, go back to my office, and call downstairs to have an administrator come up to the room. I subsequently wrote up the incident as a disciplinary referral. For his disrespect, defiance, and insubordination, the student was assigned one day of in-house suspension.

Again I ask, where is all the animosity coming from? When I was in early grade school, I was taught that when I was in a classroom, in the presence of a teacher, he or she was the boss. It did not matter if I did not like the teachers or the subjects they were teaching. My responsibility was to follow directives and always be respectful. I was not to use defense mechanisms and other ego-protecting behaviors to express my displeasure to a teacher. Such hostility is now a regular occurrence. Below is an e-mail a teacher in my department received from a student taking issue with the teacher's classroom management:

> You get in my face, attempt to intimidate me, and raise your voice all because I left class when I was suppose to. Then you lie on the write up and say that I walked out of your class with a bullcrap story. Your out to get me. I left class at 7:52 and the bell rang at 7:50. I looked at the clock multiple times before I left your class. You told the class to wait and I didn't have to because the bell had already rung so I left. You can try to lie and get me in trouble all you want but nobody is intimidated by you, I promise.

Particularly telling about the above example is not only is the student bullying the teacher but also he is bold enough to put it in writing using his school e-mail account. I did not witness that episode, but I was present for a similar incident in which a female teacher in my department was confronted.

On a Friday afternoon, as I entered a classroom to teach my period 4 class, a boy I did not know, "Johnny," came in and took a seat directly in front of the outgoing teacher's desk. This student had been escorted to the classroom by another student, "Charlie." The escort waited in the doorway, while "Johnny" immediately initiated an exchange with the female teacher in the room:

JOHNNY: Do you know me?
FEMALE TEACHER: No, should I?
JOHNNY: Yeah, you should, because you just called me a dope.
FEMALE TEACHER: So you're here to call me out on it.
JOHNNY: Yeah because you shouldn't be saying things like that.

At that point, I stepped in and tried to explain to the kid that this was a fixable situation. I asked him to step outside, but he would not even make eye contact with me. The exchange continued between Johnny and the teacher; and when Johnny saw that the teacher was not going to relent her position, he took his earpiece out, threw it to the ground, and got vulgar. ("You can't be saying expletive things like that.") At that point, a student in my class who knew Johnny came over and encouraged him to leave the room. Between the two of us, we were able to escort the student out of the room. Still standing in the doorway was Charlie, who, in my opinion, was quite pleased with the developments. It is clear that Charlie went out of his way to escort Johnny to my teacher's room and promoted the confrontation. My teacher later shared with me that Charlie was a former student of hers whom she had frequent disciplinary issues with.

The entire aforementioned scenario was precipitated by my teacher pulling Johnny aside earlier in the day for a corridor violation. Johnny did not know my teacher; but his buddy Charlie, one of the biggest miscreants in the school, held a grudge against the teacher and took advantage of Johnny's anger to add fuel to the fire. Why are such ridiculous scenarios taking place so regularly? Is there a particular stimulus that is fostering such aggressive student behavior? I believe the answer to that question is yes, and I believe that stimulus is the unbridled use of social media.

In 2014, my school district adopted a bring your own device (BYOD) policy. The culture of schools has changed dramatically as a result of the accelerated usage of the devices. The mission of the policy is meritorious. The school district recognizes that students need to be engaged in activities that promote twenty-first-century learning skills. The communication and collaboration generated by the devices could potentially contribute to the cross-curricular proficiencies students are required to demonstrate. Unfortunately, the framers of BYOD did not take into consideration the likelihood that students would interpret the initiative differently than it was intended. The policy specifically states, "The purpose of the use of electronic devices is educational." However, students have taken the position that their devices will primarily be used socially, recreationally, and frivolously. The vast majority of students are not using their devices to learn the logistics of the constitutional convention. They are not using the devices to school themselves on the proper usage of there, their, and they're. The vast majority of students are contacting other students and adults inside and outside of school department buildings, even though the policy specifically prohibits them from doing so. Moreover, what students are transmitting on their personal networks is often inappropriate, vulgar, and emotionally provocative to the point where it affects their demeanor and readiness to learn. Classroom teachers are challenged hourly by students who are emotionally charged by text they have either received or posted. The students do not put the devices away, and keep them away, upon request because they are stricken by the neurotic compulsion to allow the phones to dominate their lives. It is a serious detriment to their own individual psychology, and it is a very significant hindrance to the delivery of instruction and the ability of teachers to faithfully disseminate curriculum.

Complicating the matter is that, since 2014, there has been no concerted effort to revise the policy, enforce the parameters of proper device usage, or, at the very least, recognize that students are not incorporating BYOD into their school days in the manner in which it was intended. In addition, one of the Cranston West administrators, while being interviewed by one of our local television stations, emphatically stated, "We cannot take the phones away from them. It's part of their culture. It's part of their life." First, that administrator had no business invoking his opinion on behalf of the entire school community. Second, his grandstanding sent a clear message to the students. They have been granted complete autonomy to use their devices any way they see fit, regardless of how often instruction is interrupted, the school disrupted, and other people's rights violated. Admittedly, this is a sour subject with me because my entire life was altered because of a student's inappropriate use of technology. It's time to stop managing schools with policies that are popular and start managing schools with initiatives that are sound.

In addition to making BYOD more sound with significant revision, another facet of communication adolescents need serious instruction on is the way in which they initiate a conversation with an adult. On countless occasions, students entered my office and said, "I need you to do something for me." Being the stickler for etiquette that I am, I immediately corrected them by pointing out that, when one enters a room, one begins with a salutation. One says, "Good morning," "How are you?" or "Excuse me." One should not storm into a room and give an adult a directive. Students also fail to initiate e-mail communication correctly. They disregard an opening and closing and will write something like "Why do I have a zero posted for the test on the civil rights movement?" A course should be added to the program of studies for every high school called "Personal Etiquette and Social Protocol," and it should be a graduation requirement. Such a course would provide students insight into initiating communication properly with their teachers and classmates. It would teach them how to carry themselves appropriately in all facets of interpersonal relations and would promote greater levels of self-respect. Principal Boober does want to add new courses, but he prefers AP Chinese over an etiquette course. Although it would be extremely difficult to find a qualified practitioner to teach Chinese, Principal Boober welcomes the accolades the school would receive for having such a course more than he embraces the opportunity to foster better conduct among the student body.

Coinciding with the need to hold adolescents more accountable for their behavior is the need to promote and sustain higher standards of academic integrity. In 2017, I was directed to discuss with my department members a proposal brought forward regarding the elimination of the "F–" grade and the idea of not issuing a student a report card grade less than "50." By a tally of 15–0, those in attendance were overwhelmingly AGAINST the proposal. It was the unanimous belief of my department that those students who have such low grades tend to be the ones with excessive absenteeism, failure to make up work, and the disinclination to meet the requirements of the courses they are enrolled in. Instead of the teachers making concessions, the students should be making the necessary changes to put themselves in a more favorable position. If a student has a numerical average of "16" and a "50" is entered for a course grade, we are saying that the student did 50 percent of the work. In addition to the fact that the student did not do 50 percent of the work, it is also unfair to the other students (especially those students who have a "95"), the teachers, and the entire academic process. Other notable comments that came forward were:

> The proposal devalues hard work and dedication. Failure can and should be a motivator to improve oneself.
> We have to teach kids to work for what they want, not to manipulate the system.
> The proposal will force teachers to lie with fraudulent grade reporting. Report cards are official documents, and many teachers do not want to be associated with the falsification of such documents.
> The proposal represents poor role modeling.
> Graduating everyone hurts the academic integrity and reputation of the school.

Bill Gates said it best, "In some schools they have abolished failing grades; they'll give you as many times as you want to get the right answer. This doesn't bear the slightest resemblance to ANYTHING in real life." Many school districts are presently utilizing an Arizona-based program called Edgenuity. The mission of the program is to provide high school students with a flexible online recovery of lost credits so that they can graduate on time. The key word in that mission statement is LOST credits, not credits students are about to lose. In my school district, students who are hopelessly failing and mathematically unable to achieve a passing grade are being withdrawn from classes and eventually issued credit for the course by way of Edgenuity. A student who is carrying a cumulative numerical grade of "20," through April, is able to have that grade augmented to a "65," or higher, with one or two weeks of participation in Edgenuity. In addition, there are many students who are being allowed to substitute Edgenuity in lieu of courses that are graduation requirements. Specifically, in my school district, US history is a graduation requirement. I have more than thirty transcripts in my possession documenting that students were assigned a full credit of US history by way of a very abbreviated online option instead of the full semester course most of the other students completed. The explanation I was most often offered by the guidance counselors of those students was that they did not have room in their schedules to take a full course of US history.

Academic success is not entirely dependent upon cognitive skill and aptitude. It is also the result of personal character, integrity, diligence, persistence, conscientiousness, and self-confidence. In the same context as the aforementioned grading proposal, allowing students to manipulate the academic process devalues hard work and dedication and compromises the academic integrity of a school and its programs. This chapter has also emphasized the failure of schools to properly hold students accountable for inappropriate behavior. Just prior to this text being completed, a student at Cranston High School West, in premeditated fashion, physically launched himself into a vending machine, shattered its glass, destroyed it, and put many passersby in danger. The perpetrator made arrangements in advance to have his actions videoed. The video quickly went viral and was subsequently ridiculed at many other schools outside of the district. What once would have been an exclusionary act, and what is today still classified by municipal code as malicious destruction of property, was adjudicated casually by school administration. Neither the student nor his accomplice who videoed the incident was expelled.

However, in the next chapter, I will present the circumstances that resulted in my permanent removal from the same school.

Adolescents are astute enough to perceive when they have the upper hand. In *Lord of the Flies*, Roger kills Piggy because he knows he can do so with impunity. He knows no one on the island will hold him accountable. In many ways, Cranston West is the embodiment of Coral Island. In addition to the ineptitude of the disciplinarians, the students are well aware of the restrictions placed upon the district by the state. They know suspensions will be rare, as the data-conscious administration does not want the school's rating to decline due to an inordinate number of documented disciplinary infractions. As a result, the faculty is in a very precarious position. It is just a matter of time before someone gets seriously hurt, and I fear for the safety of my former colleagues. It's open season on teachers.

8. Beware the Ides of March

I gave my all,
but I think my all may have been too much,
'Cause Lord knows we're not getting anywhere.
Seems we're always blowin',
whatever we've got goin'.
And it seems at times, with all we've got,
we haven't got a prayer.

One person can make a difference. They can promote and enact change through their individual actions. Before he was killed on March 15, 44 BC, Julius Caesar transformed the Roman Republic into an empire. He carried out much needed reforms, including mitigating a grave financial crisis, offering relief to the poor, and introducing the Julian calendar. In contemporary American history, John F. Kennedy, Martin Luther King, Jr., and Malcolm X are all similar examples of impactful reformers. Unfortunately, in the process of inducing change, those three, and a host of others in history, became martyrs in the process. I'm no Martin Luther King, and any dream I might have had became a recurrent nightmare beginning with an episode that took place on March 15, 2019.

The start to that Friday morning was less than preferable. A wicked stomach flu had permeated the building. A large number of students and adults had contracted it, including four members of my department who were out sick. I had contracted it as well, and although I was excreting waste far beyond anything I had ever seen, I did not want to be the fifth person out in the social studies department. It was my responsibility as department chairperson to see to it that all of those classes were covered with substitute plans in place. In hindsight, I should have stayed home that day.

What is the greatest fear of the typical Cranston West student? Is it aging? Is it not getting accepted to their first college or university of choice? Perhaps it is having their BMW repossessed? The answer is none of the above. Their greatest fear is having their personal status scarred. If a teacher induces a blow to one's vanity, he or she could find himself or herself facing inconceivable consequences. Though I had no premeditated plan to challenge a student's vanity or induce a verbal confrontation with any student, my entire life would be unbelievably altered by just a few spoken sentences.

Being a Friday, and not feeling particularly well, I decided the best option was to take my classes through a formative assessment enrichment activity. It would give the students a refreshing break from the content, give them a chance to earn some extra credit, and require less exertion from myself than what normally would be needed to teach a conventional lesson. I spent $122 to initiate a new activity in two classes on this Friday. I had converted a clothing rack on wheels into a gaming prop, and I was quite excited to implement a new activity called "Concentration." During the first period class, the activity was modestly successful. During my period 3 class, lunch period, I encountered difficulty as soon as I brought the materials into the classroom.

I had a student in that class, whom for the purposes of this text I will refer to as "Stella," who had been contesting just about everything I said all week. It was a Tuesday, Thursday, and Friday class; and she had spent most of the first two days asking me, "Why do we have to do it this way?" "Why can't we just do it that way?" "This isn't fair. How come this group has three people and that group only has two?" I ignored her contentions on Tuesday and Thursday. I deduced that she was simply having a bad day or week, and at that time, her behavior did not merit a response. Given that she immediately continued the behavior on Friday, I did respond, and I have a clear recollection of what I said: "Stella, why is it that you have had an issue with just about everything that has come out of my mouth this week? Why have you been so adversarial? What is the problem?

Today, I want to take this class through a new activity, and you are already complaining. If you do not want to participate, you do not have to. There are no chains on the desk. You can stay or you can go, but please make your choice now, because you are acting very unladylike." When I reflect upon the most intense exchanges I have had with students over a thirty-year teaching career, I would not place the exchange with Stella even in the top twenty. What escalated from my choice of words on that Friday was absolutely astounding.

Stella chose to leave my class on that Ides of March Friday. The subsequent Monday, I received a call just prior to 11:00 a.m. from another teacher notifying me that Stella was zealously distributing an audio compilation of me teaching Advanced Placement psychology. I was told she was quite proud of what she created, that her mother had deemed it to be "hilarious," and that she was insisting that teachers view and listen to it. Even weeks before I told Stella she was acting unladylike, she had been secretly recording my lessons on human development, sexually transmitted diseases, and Freudian psychosexual theory. The terminology associated with those topics is quite intense and for mature audiences. Though Rhode Island has a one-way law that allows one to be recorded without consent, the recorder does not have the right to manipulate the phraseology and contents to make it look like the subject is saying and doing things he or she is not saying or doing. Stella manipulated the recordings into snippets that made it appear as if I was promoting indiscreet sexual behavior with my students, as well as making me look like a sexual maniac. This behavior was reported to the school administration; and Stella was suspended for ten days for cyberbullying, harassment, and violation of privacy.

Stella was not an ordinary student. Outside of school, she was involved in a rather prestigious event that could possibly bring her significant personal recognition. It was a potentially life-altering experience involving a cross-country excursion that she surely would have lost if the agency involved was informed that she had been suspended for ten days for desecrating one of her teachers on the Internet. Since such action could not possibly be defended, she, with unbridled support from her parents, decided to take action. Stella's parents demanded that the suspension be rescinded. To Principal Boober's credit, he held his ground and denied the appeal. The parents then went to the superintendent with a four-page indictment that Stella had supposedly written. Accusing me of inappropriate teaching practices, the main thesis of the complaint was that I was at the forefront of a "dehumanizing subjugation of females." The statement said that I had been treating people badly and behaving inappropriately for a very long time and something needed to be done about it. By district policy, once an issue lands on the superintendent's desk, building administration no longer has a role. Central administration investigates the matter and takes the action it feels is appropriate. After a relatively sedate Tuesday and Wednesday, I would find out what that action was on Thursday.

At one ten on Thursday afternoon, I had just finished my lunch and received a call from the main office secretary informing me that I was needed downstairs. I was neither surprised nor concerned about the call because, as a member of the school's leadership team, I was frequently called upon for many issues. I went to the main office promptly and found it to be barren. The lights were dim, and the entire office personnel were vacated. The principal's office door was one-third open, and I entered to find two people, one of our building union representatives and the "executive director of human resources," aka the personnel director. After a blatantly perfunctory greeting, I was quickly informed that there had been a complaint and that the superintendent was placing me on administrative leave. I asked what the complaint was but was told the matter could not be discussed. The union delegate was stunned, as he obviously was not told in advance what the purpose of this meeting was. I was then told I had to be escorted out of the building and asked to surrender my building identification card. Although I had trained myself long ago not to be surprised by anything I saw in the public schools, I was admittedly shocked. I did not understand why I had to be escorted out of the building, even if there was a matter pertaining to me that was being investigated. Certainly, I had not witnessed anything like that in my then twenty-nine years in the public schools.

I was given the opportunity to go to my office, under supervision, to retrieve my belongings. I was not thinking clearly and rather haphazardly tossed a pile of paperwork in a box. I was literally escorted to the teachers' parking lot and asked for my school keys. The personnel director told me, "We'll be in touch," and he watched from a window and made sure I got into my vehicle and left school grounds. I drove home with a somber state of mind, peering through the windshield but not seeing anything. I did arrive home uninjured, but the intensity of this event was only just beginning.

My removal from the building and the way in which it was handled caused more than a disruption. The building was in an uproar. I was no icon, but I was a senior teacher who held many roles and had twenty-four years of service to the school. The faculty was on edge, rightfully concerned about how my removal might affect them. The morning after my removal, Stella was seen entering Principal Boober's office at 8:00 a.m. In addition to being reinstated from her rescinded suspension that the superintendent described as "over the top," she also submitted a list of students SHE felt should be interviewed about my teaching practices and the way in which I interacted with students. At approximately 8:30 a.m., two central administrators were seen entering Principal Boober's office, obviously in preparation to initiate the interviews. The interviews took place in the guidance office, and my students were pulled from their classes to be questioned. The interviews took place without the presence of a union representative. Multiple students who were interviewed shared with me that they were goaded into answering a series of yes or no questions. No one was asked about the impact my class had on them or to assess Mr. Loporchio's effectiveness as a classroom teacher. Instead, the questions were clearly intended to build an incriminating dossier against me.

A full week later, while I was still in limbo, I received a call from one of the union building delegates asking for my consent to hold a union meeting. My colleagues were looking for a forum to openly discuss what had happened to me and to discuss what action they should take, if any. It was at that point that a serious mistake was made. The aforementioned union delegate I knew quite well. I had worked with him for many years, as he was one of the twelve teachers I supervised within my department. Though a very good teacher and loyal member of the department, there were instances in which he had difficulty controlling his emotions. He was the teacher who caught Stella aggressively making her video available to students and teachers. He was the teacher who referred Stella to school administration for disciplinary action. He was quite incensed by the entire scenario. I took his emotional reaction as a sign of loyalty and respect. Unfortunately, he failed to anticipate that when he informed the union president of the decision to have a Friday afternoon meeting, it would inevitably get back to the superintendent.

Why the union delegates informed the union president of the meeting I do not know. Why the union president informed the superintendent of the meeting is baffling. The protocol for discussing union matters has always been clear. No building-level or central administrators are to be in attendance for a union meeting. If they are on site, they must step out. In this instance, the superintendent was not only present at the meeting; she actually RAN the meeting. At that point, one, or preferably all the union delegates, should have assertively contested that. They did not, and the meeting was not the open forum it was meant to be. It basically involved the superintendent ordering the membership not to discuss the case because "You don't know all the facts." Though the words chosen were tactful, the message was clear. The teachers in attendance on that Friday afternoon were being told to shut up and mind their own business or they would face disciplinary action for not doing so.

I lost much credibility on that Friday afternoon. Any support I had from the teaching faculty, and the genuine concern for me from my colleagues, quickly dissipated as a result of the disingenuous and stifling edict delivered by the superintendent. With frightening alacrity, a greater number of my colleagues, some of which I worked with for many years, ceased communication with me. The ones who remained in contact with me clearly had trepidation in their voices.

Meanwhile, as the Cranston West faculty was complying with the gag order, the school calendar reached April. After many meetings and consultations with both the lawyer representing the teachers' union and my own attorney I had retained, I was summoned to the superintendent's office on April 10 for what was referred to as a predeprivation hearing, in which the accused is given the opportunity to answer to the charges. In attendance were the superintendent, assistant superintendent, the departing executive director of human resources, the newly appointed executive director of human resources, the school department attorney, the teachers' union attorney, my personal attorney, and the president of the teachers' union. Prior to the meeting, Stella' supposedly written complaint and the notes from all of the interviews conducted were made available. It was a total of twenty pages of indictments, and it was made clear to me by my attorneys that I would be expected to provide a response to every one of the allegations.

I was not at all concerned about an intimidation factor. I speak very well. I interview very well, and quite frankly, there was no one on the prosecution side of the table who possessed the ability to match my articulation. The first of the two meetings lasted two hours and thirty minutes. The topics discussed were restricted to the twenty pages of allegations. At one point, I attempted to ask a clarifying question, but was sternly informed by the school department attorney that "This is your opportunity to answer to the charges; we're not here to answer your questions." There were several interesting aspects of this hearing, most notable of which was the omission of Stella's behavior. The fact that she had been recording me for weeks, manipulated the content of the recordings, and then used her video to desecrate me in retaliation for calling her unladylike was deemed irrelevant topic at this meeting. Instead, I was responding to allegations about my behavior and things I supposedly said. I was asked if I make sexually provocative remarks to students about hot wieners. One of Stella's more outrageous contentions was that I regularly snuck around the corridors of the school sneaking up on female students and taking pictures of their behinds. I then allegedly reproduced those pictures at home and subsequently distributed copies to male students. Stella stated vehemently in her complaint that she would use her tall frame to shield her friends so that I was unable to get the pictures I was attempting to take. Stella's prevarication could not have been more obvious. In addition to being an accusation that was absolutely asinine, there were surveillance cameras in every corridor that showed no evidence of such behavior on my part.

Although the bulk of the hearing required me to respond to foolishness, I did have an opportunity to bring forth what I felt was strong and compelling testimony. First, I had all of the papers Stella had written for my Advanced Placement psychology course stored in my Google Classroom. I reproduced a set for the superintendent's perusal and flagged excerpts I thought were particularly revealing. The compositions clearly showed that Stella was a young woman of diminished mental capacity. In the very first paper she submitted, she acknowledged she had suffered from terrible anxiety her entire life. In the second paper she labeled herself a hypochondriac. "I overanalyze everything," she stated. In the third paper, she discussed terrible pain she had endured because of her parents' divorce. The papers clearly illustrated that Stella was not well, but since the superintendent declined to read the papers I had accumulated, Stella's own acknowledgement of her mental illness had no bearing on the outcome of the case.

One of the things the central administrators took great issue with was my use of sexually provocative terminology and my references to my own life experiences to teach Advanced Placement psychology. I made it clear in my opening remarks that if I was teaching Algebra I, the language would not have been so strong. However, when one is teaching about human development, psychosexual theory, and Sigmund Freud, who published text stating that sexual arousal began during the preschool years, the terminology is bound to be graphic. In what I felt was among the strengths of my performance, I used an approved AP textbook to illustrate the exact spots in each chapter where the terminology was presented. Specifically, it was the concept of sexual script that agitated the central administrators most. They refused to believe that the way in which one's lifestyle contributes to sexual behavior could possibly be a legitimate psychological topic, and they denounced the story I used to assist students in their understanding of the concept. Anything documented in the textbook could realistically appear on the spring College Board examination. In an Advanced Placement class, it is not sufficient to direct students to record definitions in notebooks without offering them the substance to truly understand the concepts. In what is a college class, students should have the intellectual capacity to handle and process the subject matter in a mature manner. The form letter that documented my reprimand stated I CLAIMED my stories were connected to the curriculum, "but were in fact inappropriate." To clarify, I didn't CLAIM anything. Claims cannot always be substantiated. I SHOWED, with references to the approved textbook, the topics I was teaching were part of the approved curriculum and that the life experiences I shared were to aid students' understanding of concepts that were being introduced to them for the first time. From September to March, no parent or student had vocalized any concern about my teaching practices, until Stella was about to lose her trip to Nevada.

I certainly expected to be called upon to discuss my actions on March 15, especially regarding telling Stella she was acting unladylike and the superintendent's preconceived conclusion that I maintain different behavioral standards for female students than I do for male students. I was asked to state my definition of ladylike. Though I possess a vast and expansive vocabulary, I do not employ terminology I do not know the meaning of. Ladylike refers to behavior that is typical and expected of a decorous female, decorous meaning refined and well mannered. The facial expressions of the prosecuting central administrators clearly indicated they were shocked I was able to state the definition without hesitation. After two-and-one-half hours and all of the allegations addressed, the predeprivation hearing ended. With the school department's spring recess approaching, it would likely be two full weeks before I knew the outcome.

On Tuesday, April 23, I was summoned back to the superintendent's office for a follow-up meeting with the understanding I would be reinstated to my teaching position the following day. The superintendent communicated her concern that I may consider seeking retaliation against Stella and perhaps the students who jumped on her bandwagon. I honestly was not thinking about Stella. Having gone twenty years straight at one point in my career without using a sick day or a personal day, I was embarrassed about my extended absence and was more concerned about my students being upset with me for not being there when they needed me. The AP exam was approaching, and students were not sufficiently prepared. My department members had gone a full month without my leadership. The final yearbook publishing deadline had passed while I was out of the building. That is precisely where my attention was when I returned to Cranston West on Wednesday, April 24.

It was the most uncomfortable day of my professional career. To start, central administration failed to tell the school I was returning. My identification badge was still deactivated, and I therefore could not get in the building. I had to wait in the parking lot for another early arrival to let me in. The substitute who was covering my classes was also unaware of my return and still on the premises. I truly never felt more apprehensive than I did on that day; and I suggested to the substitute, whom I knew personally, that he finish the week as I attempted to get my affairs in order. The circumstances that took me out of the building induced many students and adults to draw inappropriate conclusions, and I was very concerned about the reception I would get both in the classroom and the corridors. Since I had five weeks of work to catch up on, I felt it was a sound decision to have the substitute finish out the week and aim to return to teaching the subsequent Monday.

Upon returning to the classroom, I employed a business as usual approach, made a conscientious effort not to refer to my absence, and formulated a plan to somehow compensate for the missed time. Stella was not attending class. It was not the result of any request or demand I had made. She simply was not attending and was not turning in any assignments in Google Classroom. Stella was just one of 114 students in the course. My focus was on the whole, not the individual parts. I honestly felt I was able to get all four sections of the course redirected and had things moving in a positive direction. I would then make a rather startling discovery.

As I was examining the term grades from the marking period that ended during my absence, I discovered that all 115 of my grades were incorrect. The discrepancies involved more than just a point or two. Most students had been augmented five to eight, in many cases ten or more points than they actually had scored. One student achieved a grade of seventy-four, but received a ninety-three on her report card, an increment that elevated her grade from a "C" to an "A." As a department chairperson and a member of the leadership team, I considered this a very serious matter. The acceptance of my syllabus by the College Board to become certified to teach the course also included a pledge that I would carry out the mission of Advanced Placement with integrity. I therefore immediately communicated my discovery to the assistant principal for academic affairs, aka the guidance director. He invited me to his office the following morning to examine the data. Upon doing so, he acknowledged that the term grades were in fact erroneous, and then immediately attributed the errors to my substitute. The grade discrepancies may or may not have been the fault of the substitute, but I felt the central issue wasn't how the errors occurred, but what was going to be done to correct them. The administrator was unwilling to commit himself to a solution, instead telling me he would discuss the matter with Principal Boober. Before the end of the day, I received a call in my office informing me that "Theodore has decided we are not going to correct the grades." I replied, "Do you mind if I ask why?" I was told that Theodore (Principal Boober) was scared of what the parents' reaction might be, given that the report cards had already been published. I was livid.

Throughout my twenty-four years of service to the school, I saw many administrators come and go. Certainly, some carried out their duties more effectively than others. Some were more collegial than others. Some dressed better than others. All of them, however, were appropriately credentialed professionals who were appointed to their respective positions to govern the building, not to defer to parental preferences. When I communicate with administrators, I make an effort not just to discuss the problem, but also offer a potential solution. My suggestion was to draft a mass e-mail to the families involved. We would communicate to the parents that due to the absence of the teacher of record, a technical problem had resulted in inaccurate grade reporting. Having a legal and ethical obligation to report grades accurately and maintain those records in the school database, we would therefore be issuing updated report cards. I honestly felt most families would have understood the school's position and its responsibility to report and maintain accurate records. My suggestion was denounced, however, and it was reiterated that administration simply did not want to deal with the potential reaction of the parents. It was yet another odious example of a long line of instances in which the parents were granted inappropriate managerial autonomy.

As the middle of May approached, I became increasingly indignant and admittedly quite vocal about many things. In addition to being the teacher of record of 115 invalid grades, it was brought to my attention that twenty-six of my students had canceled their registrations for the Advanced Placement exam. They felt they were insufficiently prepared to succeed. It certainly was true that my absence prevented me from disseminating the complete curriculum and initiating a viable review for the test. Moreover, the school's yearbook project, which I dedicated twenty-two years to reach elite proportions, was not completed to my satisfaction. I was most incensed about the fact that for the first time in almost thirty years, the social studies department was not going to be represented at senior honors night. My absence from the building, and ineligibility to participate in school tasks, resulted in not being able to solicit nominations and purchase the awards by the required deadline. There were MANY committed and righteous students among the 115 I was assigned to, students who were not posting desecrating videos of their teachers on the Internet, who rightfully deserved to be recognized for their hard work and dedication. They were deprived of that recognition and had their senior year unfairly interrupted by foolishness. That was my position moving forward.

Of course, it did not take long for that position to reach the superintendent's office. After teaching my lunch period class on Tuesday, May 21, 2019, I was approached by Principal Boober's son, as I made my way back to my office. A very polite and well-mannered boy, he was one of the 115 students taking Advanced Placement psychology, though he was not in the same class as Stella. He presented me with a very ornately wrapped and extravagant gift of obvious expense. He thanked me for everything I had done for him. I was very moved by the tribute, but as Theodore Junior walked away, something occurred to me. The graduating seniors still had more than a week's worth of classes remaining plus final examinations. Why was Theodore Junior presenting me with a gift on this day, when I probably would see him for two additional weeks? I would have the answer to that question only thirty minutes later.

The last task I carried out for Cranston High School West was proctoring STAR Testing. While I was doing so, Assistant Principal Edith Forbes swaggered into the testing center. Completely without felicitation, she sternly approached me and said, "You've been called to the Briggs Building for two thirty." I replied that I didn't know anything about that, to which she immediately barked back at me, "I'm just the messenger. You're to be at Briggs for two thirty." At that point, I knew my career as a Cranston West teacher was over. Also rather striking was the absence of Principal Boober. Was it his responsibility to notify me that I was being removed from the building? Or was it a case that he knew my response would be less than collegial and instead he sent a subordinate in to deliver the news? In any case, it was a difficult walk back to my office. Though classes were in session, I encountered one of my best students in the corridor. Why she was in that particular spot at that particular time was very surreal. I did not want her to hear the circumstances of my removal from another source. In one of the most emotional and memorable exchanges of my career, I told her I was not coming back. I will write more about that remarkable young woman in a subsequent chapter.

Still on my way back to my office, I next encountered a teacher I had worked with for over twenty years. We had built a magnificent rapport over the years and had collaborated on many projects, and she was certainly someone I considered a friend in addition to a professional colleague. Again, I found myself having difficulty controlling my emotions as I informed her of the developments. Upon reaching my office, I crossed paths with one of my department members whom I also had worked with since the previous millennium. We embraced. I told her it was a pleasure working with her, and although a part of her might have thought I was being sardonic, I felt deep down inside she knew I was saying goodbye, not farewell.

I did report to the Briggs Building, as ordered. Upon my arrival, I was met by the president of the teachers' union. We subsequently entered a room adjacent to the superintendent's office where I was immediately lambasted. The superintendent expressed her disdain for me for what she felt was intentionally retaliating against Stella by trying to establish a constituency against her. It was certainly true that in the course of apologizing to students for my absence, I was quite vocal about that absence depriving many students of the services and recognition they were rightfully entitled to. I did not tell students to push Stella down the stairs. I did not suggest that tomatoes be thrown at Stella at graduation. I simply expressed dissatisfaction. I stated my opinion. Unfortunately, the superintendent's interpretation was different, and with Stella's parents threatening to file a lawsuit and take the story to the local media, the superintendent capitulated to their every demand. The fact that I had achieved twenty-nine years of pristine service to the school department, including a stretch of twenty straight years without taking a sick day or a personal day, was irrelevant. When I tried to speak on my behalf, I was told to "get rid of the tone." The most telling point was when the union president turned to the superintendent and shockingly asked, "Didn't the Cranston Police contact you at one point about investigating Mr. Loporchio?" After witnessing that, I pretty much knew where I stood. The superintendent stormed out of the room, and I was left with the union president. She put her hands up in the air and said, "I don't know. I am going to go into her office and try to calm her down. I will call you in an hour." I would eventually receive a call, but not from her.

Knowing I had a better chance of hitting the lottery than teaching another class at Cranston West, I went back to the school to retrieve some of my belongings after departing from the Briggs Building. I stared at the walls of what was no longer going to be my office for over an hour before driving home. Upon arriving home, it did not surprise me to have a message on my answering machine, but what I then listened to was absolutely appalling. I played a message from the executive director of human resources (personnel director) telling me I was being placed on administrative leave for the rest of the school year and emphasizing three times, "Do NOT report to work tomorrow." I found that message to be totally inappropriate. If he had something of importance to communicate to me, good or bad, the appropriate thing to do was ask me to return his call at my earliest convenience. How would he have liked it if his wife or children overheard such a message directed at him? The method he employed to "do his job" was distasteful and indicative of a person who had no comprehension of what professionalism means. It also would not be my last interaction with him.

A standard school day for me begins at 4:40 a.m. I get up, turn on the computer, look at the weather forecast, and review any headline news I want to be aware of. I try to arrive at school between 6:30 and 6:45 a.m. consistently. With the intensity and fast-paced nature of the school day, time goes by fast, unless something interrupts my regimen. With a "summer vacation" having started on May 21, I endured many sleepless nights and arduously long days. Though it was suggested that I make arrangements with personnel to retrieve the rest of my belongings from school, I could not muster up the motivation to do so for three weeks. Upon making such arrangements, I was told I could not be in the building during the school day. I was given the opportunity to go to the school at 3:45 p.m. later in the week. I made it clear to the personnel director that I had more than twenty years of materials in the building and that it would not be a fifteen-minute task to retrieve everything. The personnel director did not deem that unreasonable and did not specify any type of time limit. Within that brief conversation, he also did not mention anything regarding a change in my employment status. Two hours later, he called me back and told me that the superintendent was invoking an involuntary transfer, requiring me to "bid out" at the annual teacher assignment process, which was being held the very next day. Because I had previously been placed on leave, I was ineligible to attend the event. I was directed to find a proxy to act on my behalf. Quite clearly, I was intentionally informed of the transfer with only twenty-four hours' notice so that it would be next to impossible to contest it. I also did not have the window necessary to communicate with my personal attorney regarding any viable response. Basically, if I did not comply with the executive order, I would be considered insubordinate.

By the time I made my way to Cranston West three days later, I had already been removed from the faculty list, and the position I previously occupied had been posted to the public as a vacancy. My identification pass card was deactivated, and I could not gain entry into the building. I expected the personnel director to provide me access, most likely ask me to surrender any keys I had in my possession, and then leave and grant me the necessary autonomy to retrieve and pack the rest of my belongings. Instead, he escorted me to what was my office, pulled a desk out of one of the adjacent classrooms, moved that desk in front of the office door, and watched me empty every drawer and cabinet. After a few minutes, it became clear to him that I was not going to be able to pack everything up in twenty minutes. He imposed a time limit on me. "I can't stay here all night," he barked. Somehow, I was able to maintain my self-control and not respond to the abrasive treatment. I sent a text message to a colleague and friend (Peter) who was working late in the building. I asked him to come down and assist with bringing boxes down to the parking lot while I expeditiously tried to box the rest of my things. In the midst of a steady rain and with boxes all over the parking lot, Peter and I packed everything into our respective vehicles. Meanwhile, the personnel director sat in his Honda Ridgeline and refused to leave until Peter and I left the grounds. Either he was just being nasty, or he legitimately thought I was Spider-Man, who might scale the walls and sneak back into the building through the chimney to pilfer paper clips.

Having entered and exited the teachers' parking lot more than four thousand times in my career, the final departure, and the way in which I was leaving, was certainly hurtful. The way in which I was treated by the central administration of the Cranston Public Schools was unquestionably despicable. The original discipline carried out against Stella for desecrating me with her videos, and breaking the law in the process, was deemed by the superintendent to be "over the top." Though my actions were never the subject of a police investigation and I was neither indicted nor arraigned for anything, I was treated like a criminal. Every educator who reads this chapter should be outraged at how little support he or she may receive if faced with adversity. In my case, it was a convenient complement to the typical politics and cream so characteristic of the Briggs Building.

To this day, I maintain that everything documented in this chapter is the result of the behavior of a mentally unstable malicious narcissist, a Kardashian wannabe drama queen who believes she has a blank check to disrupt other people's lives. What makes Stella's behavior even more reprehensible is her belief that her libelist actions have made her a hero in the community. Very much like Louis XIV in French history, her motto is *L'etat c'est moi* (I am the State). She believes what she promulgates on social media offers rays of sunshine to all those desperately trying to latch onto a glimmer of hope. Use caution, Stella. The sun can warm your skin or blister it. It can nurture your flowers or wither them. It can light your path or blind you. You are traveling down a dark road.

9. Why Don't Sharks Attack Lawyers?

Their children hate them for the things they're not.
They hate themselves for what they are.
And yet they drink, they laugh.
Close the wound, hide the scar.

In 1992, seventy-nine-year-old Stella Liebeck ordered a cup of coffee from the drive-through window of a local McDonald's in Albuquerque, New Mexico. She placed the cup of coffee between her knees so she could add cream and sugar. However, as she tried to open the lid, she spilled the coffee over her lap and suffered third-degree burns. She had to undergo skin grafting and remained in the hospital for eight days. Unsatisfied with the eight hundred-dollar settlement McDonald's offered, she sued the company, claiming that the coffee was "too hot, and McDonald's was negligent about its potential danger." Liebeck's attorney had coffee comparison tests performed all over Albuquerque and provided evidence that all of the other prepared coffee throughout New Mexico's largest city was served at least twenty degrees cooler than what McDonald's was serving. Her attorney argued that McDonald's prepared coffee at 180–190°F, which was sufficient to produce a third-degree burn. If only the coffee had been prepared at a lower temperature, his client would have had more time to react and could have avoided her severe injuries.

The jurors awarded Liebeck two hundred thousand dollars in damages for her pain, suffering, and medical costs; but those damages were reduced to $160,000 because they found her 20 percent responsible. They awarded $2.7 million in punitive damages. That amounted to about two days of revenue for McDonald's coffee

143

sales. The trial judge reduced the punitive damages to $480,000. Years later, Liebeck's daughter stated that the injuries and litigation deprived her mother of having any quality in her life. Still, the case gained national attention and went to trial because a woman spilled coffee on herself after trying to balance the cup between her knees. McDonald's was never ordered to serve its coffee at a lower temperature. Such cases are often referred to as frivolous lawsuits, meaning that the complainant's claim has no merit and the case has very little chance of winning. Certainly, there are lawsuits which have seemingly ridiculous contentions; however, if someone feels they have been legally wronged, our American judiciary model allows them to pursue their claims.

According to the *American Bar Association Journal,* there are 1.35 million lawyers in the United States. Not surprisingly, New York and California have the greatest number of active attorneys. Perhaps very surprisingly, Rhode Island, the smallest state in terms of land area, employs the thirteenth most attorneys in the nation per capita. The state's Yellow Pages include more than forty pages of listings for practicing attorneys, more than any other vocation. Rhode Island is definitely among the states one is more likely to be sued in. If I feel the need for litigation, I have ample options. If I'm in pain, I can call Wayne. Among the state's 4,200 practicing attorneys, we also have a "Heavy Hitter," "A Team You Can Trust," and a firm that specifically prides itself on "solving problems."

My only specific exposure to jurisprudence during my early adulthood was jury duty. I was a seated juror on two cases, one a criminal matter and the other a civil litigation. In the criminal matter, the state brought charges against a college male for arson. The case was very brief. The state prosecutor was unable to place the defendant at the scene of the crime and was totally outclassed by the defense attorney. One thing I did take from the case was being able to say I was voir dired by a future US congressman. The civil case I oversaw was much more complicated. The case was argued for three weeks before a verdict was rendered, and it was an excellent example of how in-depth and intense the litigation can get when there is money at stake.

The plaintiff entered the courtroom and was all hunched over, as if he was looking for a contact lens. He had long suffered from scoliosis and was claiming that a car accident he got into with the defendant significantly worsened his condition. Because he was unable to work, he was claiming the accident caused undue financial hardship on his family. Moreover, the alleged physical injuries caused by the accident prevented him from engaging in all of the activities he once enjoyed with his family. The attorney representing the plaintiff asked that his client be awarded five hundred thousand dollars. The way in which that figure was arrived at was explained as one hundred thousand dollars each for the plaintiff, his wife, and each of his two children. An additional one hundred thousand dollars was requested for the family dog. Apparently, the dog had become psychologically maladjusted because the plaintiff could no longer take him for walks due to the car accident. For three weeks, numerous doctors took the stand on behalf of the plaintiff with poster boards and graphics illustrating how the impact from the accident increased the curvature of the plaintiff's spine. As a result, the plaintiff was described as now being severely disabled as opposed to the moderate disability he previously suffered from.

All of the witnesses for the plaintiff were credible orthopedic specialists and neurosurgeons. However, after hearing the testimony of the specialists called by the defense and receiving a picturesque summary of the accident, I was not convinced that the plaintiff's condition was worsened by the accident. It was made clear that the onset of the plaintiff's scoliosis was in early adolescence and that it was commonplace to advance to more serious stages during adulthood. In terms of the accident itself, the plaintiff was driving out of a store parking lot onto a main road when the accident took place. He did not have the right of way. A random element in this case was a large out-of-state truck whose driver supposedly stopped in the middle of the road and waived to the plaintiff to exit the parking lot. The testimony of that truck driver may have been valuable, but both the truck and the driver were nowhere to be found. Upon summation of the case, the attorney representing the plaintiff used a very interesting analogy to convince the jury to side with the plaintiff. He told us that, as a jury, we had power; and he claimed that power to be comparable to granting a bird flight. He actually made a very dramatic gesture with his hands simulating a bird's discovery of the power of flight. It definitely gave us something to think about before being admonished by the judge and sent to the jury room for deliberation. I was asked by the judge to be the jury foreman. It was my responsibility to lead the discussion and bring the group to a unanimous verdict. Though there was a dissenting opinion from a young juror who felt the plaintiff should be awarded five hundred thousand dollars, we were able to get him to acknowledge the finer points of the case. In the end, we all agreed that the plaintiff was using the accident to compensate for many years of pain and anguish. We awarded the plaintiff a fraction of what he was asking for. Afterward, the attorney for the plaintiff asked to speak with the jurors outside of the courtroom. He was interested in knowing what he could have done differently to achieve a more convincing argument. It was a rather fascinating opportunity to witness litigation up close and gain insight as to what motivates people to take the legal action that they do.

Motivation and money definitely came to the forefront in a most amazing case that disrupted an entire city. At the time, I was teaching at a high school of more than 150 teachers, none of us knowing that we were about to find ourselves at the epicenter of a national news story. In July of 2010, the Rhode Island chapter of the American Civil Liberties Union (ACLU) was informed about a mural addressed to "Our Heavenly Father" that was displayed in the auditorium of Cranston High School West. The complaint and subsequent lawsuit was filed by a sophomore student and self-proclaimed atheist who said the banner made her feel ostracized, out of place, and alienated. Banners bearing both the school creed and prayer were gifts from the first graduating class (1963) and were subsequently displayed in the school auditorium. The text of the prayer read:

Our Heavenly Father
Grant us each day the desire to do our best.
To grow mentally and morally as well as physically.
To be kind and helpful to our classmates and teachers.

To be honest with ourselves as well as with others.
Help us to be good sports and smile when
we lose as well as when we win.
Teach us the value of true friendship.
Help us always to conduct ourselves so as to bring
credit to Cranston High School West.
Amen.

The lawsuit was filed in April of 2011. Nine months later, a US district court judge ruled in favor of the plaintiff. In his decision, the judge stated, "No amount of debate can make the school prayer anything other than a prayer." While acknowledging that "the prayer espouses values of honesty, kindness, friendship and sportsmanship, the reliance on God's intervention as the way to achieve those goals is not consistent with a secular purpose." Five weeks later, the Cranston School Committee decided not to appeal the decision by a 5–2 vote. The banner was removed during the first week of March 2012, and the city agreed to pay the ACLU $150,000 in legal fees.

The plaintiff received much backlash from both the school and the community. She received death threats, was the subject of some very graphic postings on social media, and was openly criticized by her state representative. For a time, she was being escorted to and from school by the police and also from one class to another. She left the school shortly after she won the lawsuit to pursue public speaking events and finished up her education with her mother. In a 2014 interview, she clarified her specific motivations for taking the action that she did:

> My decision to speak out against the prayer banner came from my desire to protect the First Amendment and encourage acceptance for non-Christian individuals. I have said all along that I believe this message is one that people of any religious and nonreligious preference can support. There shouldn't have been any opposition to the prayer's removal because, when it comes

down to it, the case was not about atheism—I just happened to be an atheist. It was really about defending the right to attend a public school that did not hold a religious preference, and that right can be enjoyed by people of all backgrounds. People who wanted the prayer to remain in the school are people who do not understand that a secular government is better for all of us.

From a constitutional standpoint, the city of Cranston was not going to win the case. The banner was specifically titled "School Prayer," and there had been a multitude of Supreme Court cases that had set precedents for such a display. An option may have been to simply remove the six words which were deemed objectionable, but the president of the Rhode Island chapter of the ACLU publically stated, "It will take more than simply removing the first and last lines." I am going to take issue however with the other two motivations quoted by the plaintiff. She said the school discouraged acceptance of non-Christian individuals. I did not see that at all. During the time in which I taught at the school, we had a wide array of non-Christian students and teachers. We had Muslims, Hindus, Buddhists, and an especially large Jewish population. I cannot readily recall any scenarios or circumstances in which those non-Christian affiliates were persecuted or discriminated against. I have a greater contention for the plaintiff's claim that Cranston High School West "held a religious preference." The plaintiff was at the school for less than three years. I taught at the school for twenty-four years. I was in the auditorium often for various assemblies and programs. On numerous occasions, I was on stage to deliver a presentation. NOT ONCE was any reference made to the banner. NOT ONCE was any student asked to refer to the banner or acknowledge it. The banner was nothing more than a piece of décor from the early history of the school.

It is the early history of the school that needs to be considered when analyzing this case. It was well publicized that, just after the school opened in 1958, a student council was asked to adopt school colors, a mascot, and a school creed. Two banners were subsequently affixed in the school auditorium. That is not the entire story, however. There is much more to it. The only person who knew the entire story passed away two months before the case was decided. The principal of Cranston High School West in the 1960s was Mr. Joseph Coccia. As mentioned in chapter 3, I spent much time with him gaining information for the school's fiftieth anniversary yearbook, in 2008. Among the wealth of information Mr. Coccia provided regarding the early history of the school was the precise reason what would come to be known as "the prayer banner" was created. Mr. Coccia emphasized that the biggest challenge he saw in the early history of the school was being in the shadow of Cranston (East) High School, a crosstown icon which, at the time, was nationally recognized as one of the best high schools in the country. To compensate for a significant lack of resources and facilities, Mr. Coccia encouraged and promoted unity. The words that were eventually adopted within "the prayer banner" were meant to promote that unity and to establish Cranston High School West as its own entity. The banner was not adopted to promote religion or violate the First Amendment of the US Constitution. Moreover, the 1960s was a very turbulent time. The young school saw Cold War politics intensify with the Russians, the assassination of President John F. Kennedy, and an escalating civil rights movement. Mr. Coccia also said that, as the 1960s progressed and the first American combat troops arrived in Vietnam, the school became increasingly difficult to manage. When it became known that two Cranston West alumni were killed in action in Vietnam, administration almost lost control of the school. During those difficult times, the words of "the prayer banner" were used to instill encouragement, motivation, and comfort, not to violate the precepts of separation of church and state.

One thing was for certain. The prayer banner case totally disrupted the school. At the time, my office was adjacent to the plaintiff's US history class. I can vividly recall the police detectives in the corridors and an inordinate number of police personnel throughout the building. Anyone who has spent time around adolescents knows it does not take much for them to get emotionally charged and start jumping on bandwagons. In fairness to the students, it became extraordinarily difficult to enjoy the high school experience with the media attention the school was receiving. Yes, there were instances of people saying and doing irresponsible and misguided things, but those persons were in the minority. The vast majority of the student body was conducting itself in a commendable manner. Nevertheless, the principal at that time, Steve Knowlton, became increasingly concerned about the aura throughout the campus. Under any circumstances, he insisted on structure and order, and we did not have that during the winter of 2012. In January, allegations were brought forward by the state's largest newspaper that educational leaders were not taking responsibility to teach students civility, American history, and the true meaning of the Constitution. I was one of three teachers who volunteered to sit down with the reporter covering the story to clarify the faculty's position. I, another social studies teacher, and a science teacher, while acknowledging it was a challenge to confront the fierce emotions and escalating tension within the school, emphasized that the teachers were discussing the issues raised by the case in a productive way. In February, as the date of the school committee meeting to decide whether or not to appeal the court's decision was approaching, the turbulence in the school increased further. Mr. Knowlton felt it would be prudent for a group of speakers to address the student body. As social studies department chairperson, he asked me to be one of the speakers and attempt to enhance the students' understanding of the First Amendment and specifically the concept of separation of church and state. I told him I would be happy to help in any way I could, but I didn't feel giving the students a lecture on the First Amendment would be the best approach. I felt any words from me would be more effective if they were mostly motivational, not instructive. Mr. Knowlton allowed me to take that approach, and I delivered the following speech to all four classes on February 11, 2012. The last two paragraphs were added to the remarks I delivered to the twelfth grade class:

> Most of you know me either from having me in class or from the yearbook. You know 100 percent of my attention is focused on the stu-

dents of this school, every day, all the time, no exceptions. So I'm hoping you're willing to offer me a few minutes of your attention, not to lecture you, but to give you some information, and to commend you for the way you've conducted yourselves during a very difficult stretch we've been in.

Many years ago, in this very auditorium, I attended a faculty meeting where the principal at that time, not Mr. Knowlton, but his predecessor, made a statement to the faculty that was very nice, very thoughtful, but I didn't agree with it. He said the teachers are the greatest resource this school has. Yes, you need us to get to where you want to go. We're the lights that show you the way, but the greatest resource this school has is sitting in front of me. It's all of you. You're the ones that can make this school great. In the 1950s, the population of Cranston expanded to the point where a second high school was needed. That school became Cranston West, and it wasn't built for the politicians. It wasn't built for judges making landmark decisions, the newspaper reporters, or the protesters standing outside. It was built for you, to be part of, and to take pride in.

I can't believe the people I've been contacted by in the last month, people I don't know and never worked with, cousins I never knew I had, and a guy that when we were both in first grade actually kicked me in the mouth. They all want my opinion on "the case" and the school that they've heard is a cauldron of hostility and violence. I don't see it that way. I've experienced great things at this school from being around people like yourselves who come here Monday–

Friday in good faith to accept what your teachers are offering you.

There are, however, some things we all need to understand. First, any one of you here, and any adult, if they feel they have been personally violated, has a right to pursue it. Second, there are four guarantees in life: the first three being death, taxes, and common tasks. Fourth is the fact that every day you get up and come to school, or go about your business in the community, there are hundreds of things you can have, and hundreds of things you can't have. Sometimes we win, sometimes we lose. Sometimes things go your way, sometimes they don't. When I was in high school, my guidance counselor asked me what type of career I wanted to pursue. I told him I wanted to play shortstop for the Boston Red Sox. He paused for a moment, sat back in his chair, and said, "Anthony, you better concentrate on bringing up your geometry grade because that's not happening." My day was ruined!! But we win some, we lose some. When I was a senior, I spent a good portion of time pursuing this very popular and alluring female, just for her to write in my yearbook: "Good luck in the future if you have one." There was no Facebook or Twitter in those days, but if there was, I wouldn't have used them to threaten her or desecrate her. I didn't have to, because when I walked across the stage at graduation, my diploma was worth just as much as hers. Many of you are upset that the Patriots lost the Super Bowl. The adults in this room remember a Saturday night in October of 1986 when the Red Sox were one strike away from ending 68 years of frustration. Within seconds, however, the ball went through Bill Buckner's legs, and the potential celebration turned to misery. We win some. We lose some. We move on. More recently, I didn't win the Rhode Island million dollar lottery. I was on the phone with an insurance man who insisted I could save 15 percent on my car insurance by switching to Geico. But when I asked him to calculate the new premium, it turned about to be $111 more than I'm currently paying. That's the way it goes.

I hope you've had the opportunity in one of your social studies classes to learn about one of the greatest things ever created, and one of my favorite topics to teach, the United States Constitution. It's been updated 27 times in its history, and the first of those changes, called amendments, includes something called the Establishment Clause, saying that Congress will make no laws respecting the establishment of a religion. Although it's not specifically mentioned in the document, the concept of separation of church and state is often mentioned in the same conversation as the Establishment Clause. And you keep hearing that over and over again, separation of church and state, what does that mean? It refers to the distance between the government and organized religion. We have a situation where a judge has made the determination that the Cranston Public Schools, and specifically Cranston West, has not preserved that distance. You may not agree with that decision. You are not obligated to agree with that decision, but we have to respect that decision. As part of the legal process, the school committee can choose to appeal the decision, but the fact of the matter is, all the most notable cases involving school prayer in the last fifty years have gone in favor of the plaintiff, the person bringing forth the complaint. If the school committee chooses to appeal, they will likely lose. And if they do lose, there is a right way for you to react to that and a wrong way.

How many of you have a Facebook or Twitter account? A student asked me, "Mr. Loporchio, isn't true that I can go on Facebook and attack someone because that is freedom of speech." By attack he meant with words, not physically, but no, that is not freedom of speech. You cannot use a media source to threaten someone or post false information about them to defame them. It's called libel and it's a crime. The number of states enforcing this has quickly risen to 17 and RI could very well be next on the list. In Colorado, the first offense is punishable by up to a $100,000 fine, and, if the judge didn't enjoy his/her lunch up to 18 months imprisonment. No warning, no pep talk, no second chance. Even if you're not brought up on charges you could be sued. Rhode Island is one of the easiest states to be sued in. Is it worth it? Just for 15 minutes of fame, getting attention from your friends, or the temptation that some students can't resist to contribute to the drama of this school?

Just before the holidays many of you accepted the invitation to contribute to the Senior Directory, the portion of the yearbook in which seniors share what they've done here at Cranston West, and what their plans for the future are. This is a random page, page 242 in this year's yearbook. We have seniors here who want to open a pre-school, enlist in the military, be a physical therapist, be a nurse, be a pediatrician, teach kids music, and become a successful biologist. All of those things have something in common. They all involve helping people, and that folks is among the most admirable thing you can do in your life, help someone else who is in need. No one has stated they want to be a libelist, and hurt somebody.

In May, I'll be one of the adults who will have the pleasure of distributing awards to you at Honors Night. When you come up to the stage behind me to receive your recognition, you will do it with class and dignity, not as a libelist. A month later we will have the pleasure of watching you walk across the stage at PPAC (Providence Performing Arts Center). Whoever hands you your diploma, accept it from them with class and dignity, not as a libelist. The adults in this building care about you very much and are proud of the way you've conducted yourselves during the prayer controversy. In the coming days, weeks, and months, make us more proud. Thank you for your attention.

Six days later, the Cranston School Committee decided not to appeal the decision, the banner was subsequently removed, and the plaintiff left the school soon after. She readily pursued an out-of-state public speaking tour even though she admitted to disliking public speaking. She was the recipient of more than sixty thousand dollars of "scholarship" funds generated from endowments, trusts, and other contributions to her cause. Meanwhile, the ACLU continues to defend the right to free expression and free assembly. That is likely the rationale it uses when asked why it defends groups like the Ku Klux Klan, the Nation of Islam, and the National Socialist Party of America.

There is a problem-solving principle called Occam's razor, sometimes referred to as the law of parsimony. It states that "entities should not be multiplied without necessity." In other words, the simplest solution is most likely the right one. It is more than reasonable to assume that a compromise could have been reached in the prayer banner case. To me, it was obvious that the six objectionable words—"School Prayer," "Our Heavenly Father", and "Amen"—simply could have been removed. The remaining words were not much different from the way the school's current mission statement reads and made no non-secular inferences. Unfortunately, there was no compromise. Occam's razor was not employed. The school was unnecessarily exploited, and the episode became a media circus. In addition, the young woman at the center of the controversy came out of it with a large sum of money she had no indication she would have when she started high school. The case was far more about politics and greed than it was about the First Amendment.

The years immediately following the prayer banner case were challenging for me, but did not include involvement with attorneys. That changed dramatically in 2019 with the episode outlined in the previous chapter. When allegations are brought forth against a teacher, it is commonplace for the union attorney to preside over the case with direction from the union president. The current attorney representing my teachers' union I actually like very much personally. We are the same age. We have roots to the same childhood neighborhood. I find him to be pleasant, compassionate, respectful, and very easy to speak to. Unfortunately, a union attorney is going to proceed through a case based on the course the union president feels is best. That approach may or may not be in the teacher's best interest. Because of that concern, I took the opportunity to secure the retention of a high-profile labor lawyer who worked within a well-known firm. He was willing to take my case but made it clear he would not be able to do much until I paid him a five thousand-dollar retainer. I absolutely had to have the representation and immediately remitted the amount he requested. I was impressed with his knowledge and even more so his aggressive approach to the case. The difference between a union attorney and a private attorney is that union attorneys inevitably must give their attention to the union's position as a whole, in addition to representing an individual client. A private attorney would not be affiliated with the union and therefore could care less about the union's politics. Therefore, at the time in which

I paid to retain the private attorney, I was quite confident moving forward.

Twenty calendar days passed between being unceremoniously escorted out of my school and being provided with the opportunity to defend myself. It was during that time that I learned that the private attorney I retained knew the union attorney very well. In fact, they were once partners within the same law firm. I did not see that as a problem at all. I thought it would work to my advantage that they were familiar with each other's persona. I felt it might heighten the motivation to win the case on my behalf. Just prior to the meeting in the superintendent's office, I was allowed to use an unoccupied conference room for a final briefing with my attorneys and the union president. When my private attorney suggested an aggressive approach on a specific topic, the union president quickly interrupted him and made it clear she did not agree and sternly asserted that her approach was better because "I know the people involved here and I know how these things work." I felt it was an odd development, but I tried hard not to let it distract me or disturb my focus. I had a very challenging task ahead of me. Although I would have attorneys to both my left and right, it would be totally up to me to respond to the allegations that had been brought forth.

There is no doubt in my mind that the union president's censure of my private attorney influenced his performance in the superintendent's office. There were definitely opportunities to intervene on my behalf. Perhaps he felt that being contentious would compromise my position, but I honestly believe he was silenced by the union president's denouncement. The best example that comes to mind was during a brief exchange I had with the attorney representing the school department. He was a short older man who sat across from me with a very militant demeanor throughout the entire hearing. His posture reminded me of the way NAZI war criminal Hermann Goering looked at the Nuremberg trials as he used smug gestures to respond to the court proceedings. When I tried to ask a clarifying question, he not only refused to answer it but also went out of his way to tell me I should not have asked it. I had a response in mind, but was making a concerted effort to maintain my self-control. I thought it would have been appropriate for my private attorney to point out that I was not a criminal, we were not in a courtroom, and courtroom protocol did not apply during a "predeprivation hearing." We should have been able to have an open professional discussion, but unfortunately, the school department personnel were confused about where they were. The sign in front of the administration building says CRANSTON Public Schools, not Havana Public Schools, not Baghdad Public Schools, and not Beijing Public Schools. People in this country have the right to ask questions and object to that which they feel is wrong. Throughout the entire ordeal, that concept didn't apply to me. It only applied to two parents in the community with enough financial clout to threaten a lawsuit against the school district while simultaneously threatening the job security of the city's highest-paid employee. I hope my suspicion is wrong that my private attorney was told by the union attorney to back off because the union president wanted to handle the case in a specific way. On the chance I am correct, that would be very bad. I paid a private attorney a retainer and an hourly fee to represent my interests, not acquiesce to the union president.

As the chapters in this book have evolved, it should be clear to the readership that the case did not resolve in my favor. Throughout the subsequent summer, I consulted with other attorneys and considered further contesting my demotion and the belittlement that accompanied it. I was pretty much getting the same response every time, "Where's the union?" The final attorney I called verbally reprimanded me for inquiring about the possibility of gaining his services. He told me he would take my money as a retainer and attempt to pursue the case, but he wanted to know why I was calling him instead of the union. He said, "It has generally been my experience that the union will defend its employees. If the union is not contesting the action taken against you, they likely agree with it or don't see a reason to oppose it. If I go into a courtroom with this, understand that is likely what the judge will say and not even be willing to hear the case." Having had a lousy summer already, I certainly was not going to remain on the phone and be scolded further. It was at that point I decided to concede that my career had been annihilated and the chances of it being revived were not promising. With some of the fascinating intricacies of jurisprudence having been examined in this chapter, the only remaining question is that which titles it. Why don't sharks attack lawyers? ANSWER: professional courtesy.

10. In There with the Kids

And though it's always sweet sorrow to part,
you know you'll always remain in my heart.
Goodnight, sleep tight, and pleasant dreams to you.
Here's a wish and a prayer that every dream comes true.
And now 'til we meet again,
Adios, Au Revoir, Auf Wiedersehen.

I'm not a religious man, but I have a sound understanding of religion and spirituality. I honestly believe there are people who are heaven sent. They were put on this earth to make the world a better place and improve the lives of everyone they come in contact with. As stated in the preface, one of the goals of this book is to enlighten both novice and veteran educators on the fact that, although there are forces beyond our control that may drive us out of the profession, there are also some very good reasons to keep returning to our classrooms every September. This chapter will introduce ten individuals who changed my life. I will attempt to paint a vivid portrait of how and why each of them is so special, personifying the value of being a teacher.

A large part of my teaching dynamic involves building relationships with students. I believe in providing students with life skills and life experience reflections in addition to content knowledge. I have been fortunate to teach many special young men and women who have left a lasting impression on me. They have made me proud to be a member of the teaching profession, and I will never forget them under any circumstances. If I was fortunate enough to have children of my own, I would want those sons and daughters to be just like them. Although now pursuing their dreams and ambitions in adulthood, they are daily inspirations who give me the courage to keep striving forward, even in the most difficult of circumstances. Although they are not all personally acquainted with each other and are traveling down different roads, they all have something in common. They are the students I have taught who best understand and respect what I am as an educator: what I feel, what I value, and my feelings regarding the importance of the relationship between student and teacher. I thank them for that respect and understanding and am honored to introduce them and present their statements chronicling their post-high school endeavors.

VALERIE (Class of 2011)

I first met Valerie (Val) in September of 2007, when she was a student in my world history I honors course. By her own admission, she was never particularly fond of history classes; but she latched on to my style of teaching, embraced it, and finished the course with the grade of "A." She started high school the year we completed the fiftieth anniversary edition of our school's yearbook. In class, I often referred to that project and yearbook protocol in general. She was intrigued enough to apply for a position on the staff the following year. Val was on the yearbook staff for three years, spending both her junior and senior years in an executive capacity. As a yearbook executive, Val contributed countless hours to the project, often staying until after 10:00 p.m. on Friday nights to not only meet deadlines but to go the extra mile that would cement her place in the legacy of the project. In the twenty-two years that I advised the yearbook, there were a handful of executives who got personally absorbed in the project. They took great pride in what was being created, and it became part of them. Val was one of those persons. In a letter she wrote to me years after she graduated, her sentiment toward what she was part of was still evident. "No amount of time that passes can ever diminish the importance that being part of the Yearbook Staff has had in my life. We really created such wonderful yearbooks and put in our all. What could be more rewarding than that?"

From a personal standpoint, this young woman is the epitome of class and dignity. She has thought of me often over the years and has frequently sent me positivity, especially when I had a serious illness in the family. When my father passed away in 2017, she drove many miles from another state on an inclement December night because she wanted to pay her respects at the calling hours. That is something I will never forget. Graciously accepting my invitation to contribute to this book, she composed the following statement regarding her post-high school endeavors:

> After graduating from Cranston West, I attended Wentworth Institute of Technology, where I majored in architecture. In four years, I received a Bachelor of Science degree in architecture. I was accepted into the one-year Master's program for architecture at Wentworth following that. In 2016, I graduated from Wentworth Institute of Technology with a Master's Degree in architecture. My ultimate career choice was and is to become a licensed architect, and I am currently pursuing a license. My goal is to work my way up into a major leadership position at an architecture firm, because I love to work on a team and manage projects. I truly enjoy all aspects of architecture from design, to construction drawings, to construction administration.

An additional important development in Val's life would be her engagement. By the time this book is published, she will be married. I wish her a lifetime of good health, happiness, and prosperity. I know she will pass all of her wonderful qualities on to her children.

CHRIS (Class of 2012)

Chris was one of my students for both world history and US history and completed both courses with the grade of "A+." When I first met him in September of 2008, his assigned seat was in the back of the row nearest to the windows. He was always prepared and contributed regularly to class discussions. His conscientiousness, commendable demeanor, and capacity for good will quickly came to the forefront. I immediately saw in him the qualities I coveted for the yearbook staff. Chris was the lead executive for the school's 2012 yearbook. His extracurricular experience was totally dedicated to the yearbook. Very much like Val, he took great pride in the project and committed a tremendous number of hours to creating the best possible product for the school community. He had a magnificent understanding of my philosophy for creating yearbooks and the attention to detail that had to be present if the project was going to be successful. He and I spent a lot of time together, and it was a pleasure having him as my right-hand man. From his graduation in 2012 up until my departure from the school in 2019, Chris was an adjunct to the yearbook staff, providing technical support, assisting with production, as well as making himself available to assist with the spring distribution of the book.

There are two things that I greatly appreciate and admire about Chris. First, he is always willing to help someone in need. He has great knowledge of technology and computers. He knows all about them. In addition to being my computer technician at both school and home, he has made himself readily available to fix the computers of the vast majority of the high school staff and, in some cases, the computers of their family members. Second, his loyalty to me is the most defined I have witnessed among the more than three thousand students I have taught. When many people, including close colleagues I worked with for over twenty years, abandoned me when I became the subject of controversy, Chris remained in contact with me and continued to be on my side the entire time. I can recall a Sunday morning when I went to his apartment to pick up some computer equipment he was working on for me. His landlords asked if I was his father. I told them I would be proud if I was, but I was just a close friend. If I was fortunate enough to have a son of my own, Chris would be perfect. That is how I feel about this young man. Chris has entered a very competitive career field, but when he is provided with an opportunity, he will accomplish great things. He composed the following statement about his post-high school endeavors:

> After graduating from Cranston High School West in 2012, I pursued a degree in electrical engineering with a minor in mathematics from the University of Rhode Island. In 2018, I graduated with my Bachelor's Degree. Since then, I have continued my education and am currently pursuing a Master's Degree in electrical engineering from the University of Rhode Island. After I complete the Master's Degree program I plan on starting a career in the field of power electronics. This would include designing power grid systems for large buildings and communities as well as evaluating current systems and looking for ways to improve them. I chose this career field because I have always had a strong passion for technology and engineering. It is a very hands-on field, which is something that I look for in a career. Ultimately, I would like to make the world a better place and continue to make improvements to society. I have always enjoyed helping people, so in a field such as this, my goal is to assist communities with finding solutions to modern-day problems.

Kylah (Class of 2015)

This most remarkable young woman was a student in my world history I honors and psychology honors classes. She completed both courses with the grade of "A+" and graduated within the top five of her class. There is so much more about Kylah however that makes her inclusion in this chapter a necessity.

I have always been able to spot the special ones, and shortly after Kylah arrived in my classroom in September of 2011, I knew she would impact my life greatly. As a fourteen-year-old, she exhibited an empathy and sensitivity to other people's feelings far beyond the vast majority of early adolescents. Her thoughtfulness was unmatched, recognizing me at birthdays, Christmas, the end of the school year, and even Halloween! On April 13, 2015, I somberly walked into my mother's funeral and saw Kylah and her mother in attendance. I was overwhelmed that a student thought of me in a way that she would take a day out of school to pay her respects at the funeral and subsequent collation. It was beyond anything I've ever witnessed from a student and something I will never forget. As her graduation was approaching, she wrote me a lengthy, handwritten letter commending my teaching skill and expressing gratitude for the experiences she had in my classes while emphasizing how valuable it was to her to have gotten to know me outside of the classroom. She wrote that I had grown to become one of her close friends. The romantic poets of the nineteenth century could not have composed anything as moving.

I later received a card from Kylah's parents thanking me for "giving her the guidance and support to become the confident young lady she is today." It is I who thank THEM. Unlike some of the misguided examples discussed in chapter 6, Jack and Karen have been magnificent parents who have had a profound impact on the young woman Kylah has become. I admire Jack and Karen very much, as every day they have the opportunity to see and think about what they brought into the world. I have been able to bear witness to Kylah's evolution from her high school years to the present day, as she still keeps in touch regularly. In response to my invitation, she composed the following statement regarding her post-high school endeavors:

> After graduating from Cranston High School West in 2015, I continued my education at Providence College to study health policy and management, and business. I received my

Business Certificate and Bachelor of Science in health policy and management in May of 2019. Prior to graduation, in the fall of 2017, I had the opportunity to travel abroad to Rome, Italy where I studied theology and business. To augment my education, between 2018 and 2019, I pursued internships at Rhode Island Hospital, Women and Infants Hospital, and the Rhode Island Department of Health. Post-graduation, I accepted a full-time administrative assistant position for Lifespan Physician Group. In tandem, I am pursuing my Master's Degree in healthcare administration at Suffolk University and plan to graduate in May of 2022. In the future, I aspire to further my education and work in the quality-improvement sphere in either a hospital or government setting. This career path will help me reach my professional development goal of making a meaningful impact on the healthcare system by improving the health and welfare of the public.

Jensen (Class of 2017)

This young woman was a transfer student from another high school. I was fortunate that the tides brought her to my psychology class during her senior year. Completing the course with the grade of "A," Jensen was always the most actively involved and emotionally absorbed in the topics that were being taught. She clearly recognized the power of psychology and how what she was learning could serve her well throughout the career she would be pursuing. Jensen is a very verbal young woman. She enjoys engaging with people, and she herself is very easy to speak to. I very much enjoyed our talks on a wide variety of topics both in school and out of school, as she has made a concerted effort to stay in touch since her 2017 graduation.

An avid baker, Jensen has frequently brought me brownies and muffins for Christmas, because, as she wrote to me, she considers me as magical as the holiday season.

When teaching an average of 80–120 students per year, the impact I am having on any one my students is not always readily visible in the classroom. However, when I read what Jensen wrote in my yearbook, I was thrilled that my teaching dynamic and the power of the subject I taught her affected her in a very profound way. She wrote, "Thank you for everything you've done for me. Without you, I would have never figured out what to do with my life. I will miss your stories and our talks. Thank you for always giving me a place to go if I was upset or just wanted to talk. You're amazing!"

Jensen has definitely figured out what to do with her life, though at the moment I am writing this, I am quite concerned about her well-being. She is currently in Europe in the midst of the coronavirus pandemic. Before embarking on her journey, she composed the following statement regarding her post-high school endeavors:

> Since graduating from Cranston West, I have been studying at Quinnipiac University in Hamden, Connecticut. I am pursuing a Bachelor's Degree in public relations and journalism with a minor in sports studies. I was also accepted to study abroad in Florence, Italy for the spring 2020 semester. After graduating from Quinnipiac in the spring of 2021, I plan to work in either the healthcare or sports industry of public relations. I love event planning, talking to people, working with the community, and showing off what I can accomplish to help others. I chose public relations because it was something I always found interesting. To be able to help people, whether it being planning a charity event or promoting someone's business, I am all for it. Being able to work in this field while also doing something good for others is a dream come true.

Lilit (Class of 2017)

It is compassion that separates man from beast. That fact could not be more evident in the persona of this young woman whom I first met in September of 2013. Lilit, or "Lilo" as she is affectionately known, was a student in my psychology honors class. Completing the course with the grade of "A," she was among the most defined examples of a student who understood the finer points of my teaching dynamic. While being actively engaged and absorbed in the subject matter, she found my stories, idiosyncrasies, and quirks to be very endearing, to the point in which she would often quote me in and out of class. Like all of my other students being introduced in this chapter, Lilit's character shines just as brightly as her academic prowess.

Lilit is a very spiritual young woman who holds an ardent fervor for her Armenian heritage. She spends many weeks each year in what she refers to as "the motherland," and I am inclined to believe that she would like to move there permanently someday. Meanwhile, to celebrate her motherland, she frequently brings me *gatas*, an Armenian pastry and sweet bread often filled with flour, butter, and sugar. Lilit was a CNA at the nursing home in which my father resided. Though my father inexplicably introduced himself as "Chico," they developed a very nice rapport. In a wonderful demonstration of compassion and good will, Lilit spent much time with my father, seeing to his needs, comforting him, and attempting to boost his spirits. Lilit believes that everyone should have a nice birthday, and she was able to goad my father into revealing mine. When that day arrived, she somehow was able to get into the school building at 6:00 a.m. and decorated my office door and corridor with birthday regalia, so that I would have a very out-of-the-ordinary surprise upon my arrival. It was as amazing as Lilit herself.

Whether it is in Rhode Island, Armenia, or somewhere in between, Lilit is unquestionably a young woman who will make this world a better place. Graciously accepting the invitation to contribute to this book, she composed the following statement regarding her post-high school endeavors:

After graduating from Cranston High School West in 2017, I then enrolled at the University of Rhode Island and majored in cell and molecular biology as a pre-health student. My academic and professional experiences led to becoming a Pre-Health Ambassador during my sophomore year at URI, mentoring 20 freshmen for their college and career pursuits. During this time, I was employed at Cedar Crest Nursing Center in Cranston, RI as a receptionist, scheduler, and dietary aid. I was also a medical scribe in the Emergency Department at Landmark Medical Center in Woonsocket, RI part time. Volunteering plays a major part in my life. I volunteered at my church—aided in visiting local nursing homes, women's battered shelters, and schools. I had the honor of volunteering at Hasbro Children's Hospital where my late brother Felix spent a lot of his time. There, I was the leading assistant for the 5th floor playroom and took part in strengthening reading and writing skills of the young patients. I enjoy taking frequent trips to Armenia during the summer where most of my family is located. During my last trip, I was engaged in an externship at Nork Marash Medical Center, shadowing an anesthesiologist for cardiac patients. What I love most about Armenia is the warm, good-hearted people I meet and the unique, historical background of the land itself. I currently reside in Los Angeles, California where I am excelling in my professional goals at the Smidt Heart Institute at Cedars-Sinai Medical Center. I work alongside surgical residents and administration as an administrative/research support assistant. I am awaiting acceptance to various Californian universities where I will continue to major in biology. My focus is to prepare myself for medical school, with a specialty in oncology, and be of aid to my community, as the doctors and medical caretakers did for my brother.

Sophia (Class of 2017)

This young woman is a magnificent example of a student who utilized every opportunity her school provided her to grow academically and socially. I was privileged to know Sophia as both a student in my psychology honors class and a member of my yearbook staff. She completed my course with the grade of "A+," as part of a transcript that resulted in her being designated the salutatorian of her graduating class. Sophia held a sincere appreciation for the educational process and the roles her teachers played in her academic career. She posted in her senior yearbook, "Without the support and dedication from my teachers, I would not be where I am today. I believe the challenges and experiences that my teachers set forth greatly influenced my success socially and academically." Sophia was on my yearbook staff for four years and served as a lead executive during her junior and senior years. In that capacity, she maintained an undying respect for my philosophy regarding how a yearbook should be produced. She enthusiastically and diligently contributed to the success of the project and heightened her leadership skills in the process.

Sophia was one of many students very much distressed by my removal from the school. Because her younger sister had me that very year, she was very well aware of what was transpiring. On her own initiative, she composed a two-page letter and sent it to the superintendent. In that letter, Sophia articulated her position very effectively. It was written with conviction, especially in regard to my teaching style and enthusiasm for my subjects, the way I handled myself in a kind, courteous, and professional manner, and the way I consistently thought of others before myself. The most potent statement of the composition was "I believe that it is extremely unjust to disassemble the respect, integrity, and contribution Mr. Loporchio has provided to the Cranston West community with unreliable statements from a student with a contestable reputation." Sophia received a five-word perfunctory answer to her letter. Perhaps if she threatened to file a lawsuit against the school department the way in which Stella's parents recklessly did, she would have received a more thoughtful response. Nevertheless, the fact that Sophia took the initiative to write such a letter clearly showed her superior character. Furthermore, the statement she composed for this chapter unquestionably illustrates her mission to accomplish great things:

> After graduating from Cranston West in 2017, I advanced to Boston College to pursue a Bachelor of Science degree in biology on the pre-medical track. I am currently working to apply for a minor in Global Public Health and the Common Good. My time at Boston College has been filled with many memorable experiences including two service trips through Habitat for Humanity as well as an international cultural immersion trip to Costa Rica. Academically, I have also engaged in the opportunity to be a teaching assistant for the introductory biology laboratory course offered at Boston College. I plan to apply to medical school following the completion of my senior year and work for a full year prior to resuming my education. In that time, I anticipate working in the field of public health in order to continue to develop my intrapersonal skills and expand my experience and understanding of patient care and population health. A career in medicine has been a steady goal since high school because it reflects my ever-growing interest in the sciences and humanities. It is rewarding to know that I am pursuing a profession that continuously promotes personal

development and the advancement of interdisci-
plinary knowledge.

Madison (Class of 2018)

I unexpectedly met Madison during her sophomore year, when she was making up a test for another teacher. Upon completing that task, she was introduced to me, and she shared her interest in taking Advanced Placement psychology. She was the recipient of effusive praise from her teacher who was certain she had the scholastic aptitude and maturity to excel in the course. Madison did take AP psychology as a senior. The aforementioned praise turned out to be an understatement, as this young woman is an absolute gem.

As summer assignments were being completed by way of Google Classroom, Madison's name was not appearing on any of my three class rosters. Fortunately, I was able to reach her by way of e-mail, and she was able to resolve the scheduling snafu. She responded, "Don't worry. I'm definitely taking the class!" Madison completed the course with the grade of "A+," scored proficiently on the Advanced Placement exam, and was the recipient of an award at senior honors night for excellence in AP psychology. More importantly, she communicated to me that the class was very valuable to her. She was especially appreciative of my positivity, support, and effort to teach Advanced Placement without inducing unnecessary stress upon the enrollment. Just hours after graduation, she sent me an e-mail commending the speech I delivered and thanked me for attending the event. She wrote that she felt supported by my presence. Though she was away at college, she gained knowledge of my removal from Cranston West and was quite indignant about it. She obtained my personal e-mail from an unknown source and sent me the following communication:

> Good Evening Mr. Loporchio:
> I hope you don't mind that I reached out to
> a student for your personal e-mail. I needed to
> get in touch with you and I wish I could've done

so sooner. I am utterly disgusted and disturbed to hear of the situation you have been put through this school year. I know there is nothing I can say or do to change what happened but I offer my sincerest apologies. I don't want this event to ruin you. Please be assured when I tell you there are countless students who see how unjust this is. Many of those are so thankful for the person you are and the experience you have provided us with. You were definitely the teacher who had the most positive impact on me all throughout high school and I am very thankful for that! Thank you for all the wonderful, kind, and selfless things you have done for your students. They won't ever go unappreciated—especially by me! I have been thinking about you and keeping you in my thoughts and prayers. Please do me a favor and take care of yourself. You deserve the best. If you need anything please don't hesitate to reach out.

I was very moved by what Madison wrote, but not at all surprised. She is a very religious young woman. In fact, she postscripted the above communication with Proverb 11:9, "With his mouth the godless man would destroy his neighbor, but by knowledge the righteous are delivered." In addition, Madison has very maternal instincts. On many occasions, when she submitted essays for my class related to parenting and childhood, she often mentioned the unconditional love she already holds for her future children. She will indeed be a terrific parent and wife, and since she will also be a magnificent daughter-in-law, I wish I had a son her age. Graciously accepting my invitation to contribute to this book, she composed the following statement regarding her post-high school endeavors:

I am currently attending Salve Regina University. I am a nursing major and a Spanish minor. After I graduate in 2022, I am immediately attending graduate school in order to become a certified nurse practitioner. The end goal that I have in mind, which has been the same throughout high school, is to become a neonatal nurse practitioner, a bilingual one of course. The Neonatal Intensive Care Unit is the unit in the hospital for infants born premature, sick, and/or addicted. It is the job of health care workers there to stabilize them and watch over them until they are healthy enough for their families to take them home. Essentially, I will be both a health care provider and a temporary parental figure while these infants' parents are unable to take care of them. It is a demanding job that I know will be packed with days of both triumph and tragedy, but I have no doubt that it is my calling in life!!

Nickolas (Class of 2019)

Nick was one of 115 students enrolled in Advanced Placement psychology for the 2018–2019 academic year. I had no previous contact with Nick, but he quickly emerged as one of the most vocal participants in the course. He consistently asked questions, brought forth his viewpoint on many of the topics, and made a positive contribution to every class. There were an unprecedented four sections of the course, and each class had its own personality. Though I felt I had established a positive rapport with all of them, it was Nick's class that I bonded with the most. It was the group that found my teaching dynamic and mannerisms the most endearing. There was a student in the class who frequently wore a snorkel. I would tell her how popular those jackets were when I was in early grade school and how exciting it was to see them making a comeback. I would jokingly tell her to put her hood on so she could be "comfy and cozy." During a class just prior to the Christmas vacation, Nick asked me if he could go to his locker to get something. I prefer that students not go to their lockers during class, but when Nick told me it was "very important," I allowed him to go. Upon his return, he presented me, on behalf of the class, a shopping bag containing a snorkel. It was an unforgettable moment in my career. The present was from the entire class, but Nick was clearly the driving force behind it. I taught the remaining minutes of the class wearing the snorkel, even though it was seventy-one degrees in the room.

I enjoyed teaching all four classes that year; but as the year progressed, it was Nick's class, my period 2 RED, that I enjoyed interacting with the most. That enjoyment came to a thudding halt when I was removed from the building on March 21. Thereafter, Nick was one of my strongest supporters among my students. He made frequent attempts to discuss the situation with administration, and he initiated an assemblage of student signatures on a petition calling for my immediate reinstatement. Like receiving the snorkel, I was overwhelmed by a student taking such action on my behalf. It was later brought to my attention that Nick was threatened by Stella's father at his place of employment because he was advocating for me so fervently. I very much regret that he had to endure that, but he was mature enough to use the incident to gain a better understanding of Stella's actions. Atrocious actions by parents often result in their children behaving heinously.

Nick later shared with me why he respected me to such an extent. In addition to his regard for my teaching and dedication, he had a personal experience that was very similar, one in which he was unfairly accused of misbehavior. He and I had many conversations about that and many other facets of life. I am confident he considers me a friend and an advisor. He was very excited to receive my invitation to contribute to this book and composed the following statement regarding his post-high school endeavors:

> Post Cranston West, I am attending the University of Rhode Island, and am currently in the Computer Science program, which I am majoring in. I also plan to minor in cyber security. Though the field reaches a numerous range

of occupational areas, my ultimate goal is to work somewhere within a clandestine area of the government. Aside from the growth and potential the major demonstrates, defending the country in an impactful and modernized way is what I have always dreamed of. Cyberattacks are the new warfare, and if I can uphold the existence of America, I will feel a true purpose in my life that I have always longed for.

Gabrielle (Class of 2020)

At a time when so many students are coming into high school steeped in vanity, self-centeredness, and egocentrism, it is refreshing to meet students who are the epitome of those we wish to graduate. That description certainly applies to Gabby, who was a student in my world history I honors and Advanced Placement psychology courses. After completing the first course with the grade of "A+" and winning a Spider-Man action figure in one of my formative assessment activities, she was excited to have me again for AP psychology. Fortunately, she made the decision to take the course during her junior year, as I would not be on the faculty to teach the course during her senior year. In AP psychology, Gabby replicated her previous academic excellence with another "A+" and was one of the most proactive of learners among the 115 students enrolled. I look upon Gabby as much more than just an "A+" student. Especially in the psychology class, she made definitive connections with the subject matter and was emotionally moved by the stories I shared about my life. I honestly believe that her reaction to my teaching style and persona is the primary reason she and I have the rapport today that we do.

Gabby was one of the first persons to reach out when I was removed, and she has stayed in touch to this day, including trekking across the city on a busy Friday afternoon to visit me at my new place of employment. In addition, she drafted a full-page letter to the superintendent describing her experiences in my classes and requested a meeting at the superintendent's convenience to discuss the matter further. Since there were many students who were pulled out of their classes and confronted with yes or no questions about my teaching, Gabby and several of her classmates felt they should also have the opportunity to share their thoughts, insight, and assessment of my teaching. Gabby was not granted the courtesy of a response. She was, however, honored to accept my invitation to contribute a statement to this chapter regarding her post-high school endeavors:

> I was accepted to the University of Vermont, University of Rhode Island, University of Connecticut, University of New Hampshire, and Providence College. After staying at UVM, my top choice, for two nights, I obtained a very accurate depiction of the student life and type of person that embodies a UVM student. The care-free, non-judgmental and welcoming nature that the students possess is the main attraction I have towards the school, as I feel I possess those same qualities. Taking AP Psychology certainly helped me acquire a great understanding of my own thoughts and actions, as well as those of people around me, shaping me into an understanding and level-headed individual. For that reason, I will be attending UVM, where I will be studying political science with the ultimate goal of going to law school to eventually work as a lawyer. I strive to use my well-developed analytical skills to achieve justice in any particular situation. My heart goes out to people who do not have the ability or confidence to speak up for themselves, particularly in cases regarding children. As a law-yer, I will make it my mission to achieve justice for those who are truly deserving of it.

Rachael (Class of 2020)

She's academically driven. She's passionate. She's determined. She's ethical. She's empathetic. It is absolutely no exaggeration that Rachael is among the most spectacular persons I have ever had the privilege to instruct. I actually first met her during her sophomore year as a result of misspelling her name on a plaque she received for excellence in Advanced Placement US history. The fact that she received that accolade for a class with a predominantly junior enrollment was a preview of the academic imprint she would indelibly place upon the school. She took my AP psychology class as a junior and consistently exhibited exemplary qualities that set the perfect example for her classmates to follow.

Rachael has the energy of a dynamo, is never at a loss for words, and has a wide array of knowledge ranging from biology to the Boston Red Sox. I am impressed the most by the way in which Rachael exhibits a wisdom and maturity far beyond her chronological age. I am inspired by every conversation I have with her and every e-mail I receive from her. It is remarkable that the following text was written by a seventeen-year-old. Filled with compassion and empathy, how could I not be uplifted by it?

> It makes me so happy that I am able to inspire you and help you move forward from such an unwarranted and degrading experience. I know that 2019 wasn't your happiest or most successful year, but it is one of my resolutions to make sure that your 2020 tops it by a great margin. No one deserves the treatment that 2019 served you, especially someone of your caring, thoughtful, and kind-hearted nature. I hope that in 2020 you begin to feel the self-satisfaction that you had before last year's incident, and realize that one person cannot take away your accomplishments or character.

A day automatically gets better when Rachael becomes part of it. During the college application process, I felt so strongly about this young woman that, in addition to composing her college recommendations, I called the admissions office of her top school of choice to speak to a representative on her behalf. I wanted to do whatever I could to enhance the candidacy of this extraordinary young woman so she can pursue her dreams. I am thrilled that this book gave me the opportunity to write about her and this gave the book's audience the opportunity to read Rachael's statement regarding her post-high school endeavors:

> Since as long as I can remember, I've longed for the opportunity to explore. The discovery of a location's secrets and never-before-seen nooks and crannies infatuates me. Aligning with this adventure lust, I've known for quite some time that I want to attend college out of state. Over the course of two years, I visited 17 schools. Those visits were followed by the ever-dreaded application season. However, I can honestly say that the stress and agony involved with the process paid off, as I was accepted to Vanderbilt University, Georgetown University, the University of North Carolina at Chapel Hill, Villanova University, and the University of Miami. My current top contender is Vanderbilt University, due to their academic rigor and status, an ideal location in Nashville (the country's fastest developing city), and prominent social life. I intend to double major in neuroscience and psychology in hopes of engaging in neuropsychological research.
>
> As many teens do, I struggled to choose my major. I am a Type-A student to the core so this lack of a stable plan severely bothered me. Only when I took AP Psychology in my junior year did I realize my love for the subject and my desire to

continue exploring it throughout my life. I had Mr. Loporchio as the teacher for that class and he fostered my interest, taking time outside of class to discuss the content with me and career paths associated with the subject. As I began to do more personal investigation of the subject, including reading psychological articles and learning about psychological experiments online, I developed a deeper appreciation for the field and for the opportunities to thrive in it, while simultaneously expanding it.

I discovered my passion for service and for bettering the local and global community when I traveled to an orphanage for severely disabled children halfway up a mountain in Montego Bay, Jamaica in the summer of 2019. I stayed at the orphanage for a week with a group of ten other teens. The residents of the orphanage live in strained conditions and battle autism, cerebral palsy, Down syndrome, spina bifida, and sensory ailments. Throughout the week, I fed them 3 times a day. I also read, colored, sung, and danced with them, helping to improve their intellectual and social skills. As the presiding artist in my group, I additionally did arts and crafts with the residents and painted an approximately 12'x72' mural at the gates of the campus. By the end of my trip, I'd adapted to third-world-country habits and, hence, gained empathy for those who must practice these conservative techniques every week of their lives, not just one. Never again will I take my life for granted, as I have all that the residents could want, the opportunity to learn, travel, choose my future, and walk, talk, and see. I am forever grateful that I got to spread my talents across the world and impact the lives of others. I'll never forget the unwavering smiles of the residents or the connections I formed with them and my fellow missionaries.

Now that I am in college, it grows more difficult to appreciate life's simplistic wonders. The looming questions of my undetermined path have me thinking of the future more than the present. While my trip to Jamaica didn't alleviate all of my worries about my prospective responsibilities, it taught me to value life's nuances."

Being "in there with the kids" is the most valuable component of the teaching profession. Although ten of my former students were the focus of this chapter, I have taught more than three thousand young men and women in my career. Many of them have distinguished themselves in a very positive manner. There will always be some misguided individuals. Though it is true that evil sometimes triumphs over good temporarily, it never permanently conquers. No act of malice can eliminate the quality of what I have achieved with my students or what my students have achieved with me. I know that Val, Chris, Kylah, Jensen, Lilit, Sophia, Madison, Nick, Gabby, and Rachael will put forth the same effort as I will to always reserve a place in our hearts for the richness of what we experienced together.

Epilogue

Moving My Cheese

In 1998, American physician Dr. Patrick Spencer Johnson published *Who Moved My Cheese*, about the different ways we respond to life's changes and how doing so skillfully can help us find more success and happiness in our lives. The story centers around four main characters and a large, twisting maze. The cheese is a metaphor for the things we value most in life: health, family, spirituality, a career, and perhaps even material possessions. The maze represents our families, employers, and the communities we live in where we look to achieve our greatest success. Psychologically, we tend to dwell on what WAS, instead of embracing what IS. The central message within Johnson's ninety-two pages is that change is inevitable. If we learn to adapt to change, we will ultimately gain more satisfaction and fulfillment in both our personal and professional lives.

I've been encouraged by many people not to be fixated on what happened. "Let it go! You're still working. You still have healthcare. You're making top step. You're better off someone else," they tell me. If I'm coming across as fixated, it's because it hurts. When one loses a loved one, it hurts. If one is forced to put their dog down, it hurts. When passion, dedication, and commitment result in desecration and ostracism, it hurts. What I was involved with was very important to me. As frustrating as it could be to be a Cranston West teacher, I experienced a lot of memorable things there. Quite frankly, the best things I've done in my life were at that school. When I was informed

I would no longer be there, it hurt. The way in which the entire situation was handled by the school department administration was beyond egregious. The individual student who was the catalyst for my demise lives a life of reprehensible, unbridled malice, unfortunately illustrating that kindness, compassion, courage, ethics, and even love cannot always save us.

Nevertheless, as I am composing the final sentences of this book, I feel both cleansed and satisfied that I have told my story. I have presented the warning signs for teachers to look for to hopefully avoid falling victim to the same predicament. Most importantly, this book provided the opportunity to introduce ten of the finest young adults there are in this world, true inspirations that should immediately come to mind if someone asks you, "Why do you stay in it?" Sniff, Scurry, Hem, and Haw all rediscovered their cheese. Perhaps one day I will as well. Please enjoy yours.

CPSIA information can be obtained
at www.ICGtesting.com
Printed in the USA
LVHW032349100121
676157LV00002B/484